This woman is incomparable. Jennifer's words here are like being wrapped up in the kindest embrace of tender grace and handed a steaming cup of tea for your parched places. These pages will deeply comfort you, make you laugh—and let you just exhale and feel the relief of not *having* to carry it all. We are loved and cupped and carried in the most perfect hands of all—His—and He's got the whole world in His hands and under His trustworthy control. *It's All Under Control* is the gift your soul has been desperately seeking—to feel how His arms of love are under you, carrying you through it all.

ANN VOSKAMP
New York Times bestselling author of *The Broken Way* and *One Thousand Gifts*

It's as if Jennifer has been inside our heads. She knows what a trap control is, and with practical steps, humor, and insightful study of Scripture, she leads us to a biblical view of how to release control in our everyday lives to a very real and reliable Savior.

RUTH CHOU SIMONS
Artist and bestselling author of *GraceLaced*; founder of GraceLaced.com

If you're a control freak like me, beware: this book hits hard. I speak from experience when I say that this book will get up in your business and unwrap your white knuckles from around all the things you're trying to micromanage. And it will be the very best thing that's ever happened to you.

LISA-JO BAKER
Bestselling author of *Never Unfriended*

We all have our camouflage techniques, our clever disguises, and our well-formulated justifications about why the world just won't spin quite right if we resign as Fixer of Our Own Universe. Thank God that Jennifer has read our proverbial e-mails and written a compassionate road map to lead us out of our infernal striving, moving us from inner exhaustion to trusting rest. And she doesn't point the way from her lofty theological perch. She takes our hearts gently as a trusted friend and guide. If you've ever needed a place to send in your resignation as Queen of Making Sure Things Totally Beyond My Control Still Turn Out Right—start here.

ANITA RENFROE
Author and comedian; recovering control freak

I've tried so hard for so long to be the perfect wife, mom, and friend—only to feel empty and desperate. We can give up control and discover a new way of living and loving. Sounds easy, but *how*? It happens one brave step at a time. Page after page in Jennifer's book spoke directly to my heart. If you want change, this book is a perfect first step.

LISA LEONARD
Jewelry designer and writer

We live in a time when there seems to be a way to control and track every move of our lives. Jennifer Dukes Lee understands just how overwhelming this can be for the hearts of today's Christian women. When it feels like the weight of the world is on our shoulders, *It's All Under Control* offers hope for the woman who wants to entrust it all to the hands of Jesus. For the woman who feels like it's up to her to make sure everything goes well, for the woman who struggles to say, "I need help," for the woman who is so busy, loving her family so well, that she feels like she is rushing right past Jesus, this book is a practical and powerful guide to living free.

BECKY THOMPSON
Author of *Hope Unfolding, Love Unending,* and *Truth Unchanging*

Jennifer is a weaver of words and a master of metaphors—and she's done it again in her third book. If you constantly carry around anxiety and stress because you're afraid something won't go according to plan, this book is for you! In her gentle but powerfully convicting style, Jennifer gives you tools and inspiration to help you let go of your need to try to control and micromanage your life and everyone else's life. In this refreshingly honest book, you'll discover how to find freedom from being a control freak.

CRYSTAL PAINE
New York Times bestselling author of *Say Goodbye to Survival Mode*; founder of MoneySavingMom.com

If you'd asked me, I would have said I don't struggle with control. And I would have been wrong. This book gave me a key I didn't even know I needed, one that has helped set me free from stress, pressure, and anxiety. Jennifer's wise, powerful, encouraging words are a must-read for every woman who has ever felt weary or overwhelmed—especially if you don't understand why or what to do about it.

HOLLEY GERTH
Bestselling author of *What Your Heart Needs for the Hard Days*

Jennifer Dukes Lee uncovers a pressure-relieving revelation few of us have ever considered—that we don't need to hide, squelch, or alter who God created us to be, but instead rechannel our gifts and our desires in order to experience unprecedented, profound inner peace. *It's All Under Control* shows us how to stop pushing, proving, hustling, and controlling so we can begin partnering with God to honor the beautiful plan He has for our lives. It is a life of meaning, peace, purpose, and love that far surpasses anything we could have ever planned on our own.

RACHEL MACY STAFFORD
New York Times bestselling author of *Hands Free Mama, Hands Free Life,* and *Only Love Today*

In a world where hustle is king, the healing words on these pages are a breath of fresh air. It's a poignant reminder to take God off your to-do list, make him a part of your every day, and learn to let go—living life according to his plan. *It's All Under Control* will turn you inside out, check your heart, change your perspective, and help you discover that it *is* all under control because God's got this.

KARIANNE WOOD
Author of *So Close to Amazing* and *You've Got This (Because God's Got You)*

Control is an illusion. That was the message I heard as I began this book, and it's the message God confirmed again and again through Jennifer's words in *It's All Under Control.* I wasn't three pages in before I was overcome with Holy Spirit chills. For every woman who is paralyzed by fear of the future or overcome by anxiety trying to orchestrate today, *It's All Under Control* is convicting, life-changing, and peace giving.

ERIN ODOM
Author of *More Than Just Making It* and *You Can Stay Home with Your Kids!*; creator of *The Humbled Homemaker* blog

*A journey of
letting go, hanging on &
finding a peace you almost
forgot was possible*

It's All Under Control

Jennifer Dukes Lee

TYNDALE
MOMENTUM®

The nonfiction imprint of
Tyndale House Publishers

Visit Tyndale online at www.tyndale.com.

Visit Tyndale Momentum online at www.tyndalemomentum.com.

Visit Jennifer Dukes Lee at jenniferdukeslee.com.

TYNDALE, Tyndale's quill logo, *Tyndale Momentum*, and the Tyndale Momentum logo are registered trademarks of Tyndale House Publishers. Tyndale Momentum is the nonfiction imprint of Tyndale House Publishers, Carol Stream, Illinois.

It's All Under Control: A Journey of Letting Go, Hanging On, and Finding a Peace You Almost Forgot Was Possible

Designed by Eva M. Winters

The author is represented by the literary agency of Alive Literary Agency, 7680 Goddard St., Suite 200, Colorado Springs, CO 80920, www.aliveliterary.com.

For information about special discounts for bulk purchases, please contact Tyndale House Publishers at csresponse@tyndale.com, or call 1-800-323-9400.

Library of Congress Cataloging-in-Publication Data
Names: Lee, Jennifer Dukes, author.
Title: It's all under control : a journey of letting go, hanging on, and finding a peace you almost forgot was possible / Jennifer Dukes Lee.
Description: Carol Stream, Illinois : Tyndale House Publishers, Inc., 2018. | Includes bibliographical references.
Identifiers: LCCN 2018015077| ISBN 9781496430465 (hc) | ISBN 9781496430472 (sc)
Subjects: LCSH: Christian women—Religious life. | Providence and government of God—Christianity. | Simplicity—Religious aspects—Christianity.
Classification: LCC BV4527 .L4454 2018 | DDC 248.8/43—dc23 LC record available at https://lccn.loc.gov/2018015077

Printed in the United States of America

25   24   23   22   21
 8   7   6   5

To Scott,

my favorite farmer, the one who taught me
that, no matter what, "God's got it."

Contents

〰〰〰

Introduction

ᗷᗷᗷ

I wrote this book for a woman I know.

She wants a life of meaning. She wants to know her purpose. She wants to love and be loved.

But she is tired.

What exhausts her? Directing outcomes, overhustling, and managing the impressions she leaves on people. She can't let go of a nagging fear about her future and the prevailing belief that she needs to be the most responsible person in the room.

She is tired, yes, but she doesn't know how to stop.

This is what she does—she keeps it all under control, and she is under control, *thank you very much.* Smiling, even in the trenches. And always, *fine, just fine.*

"I got this," she says. And a lot of people believe her.

But she doesn't "got" this. Her outward fine does not match her inner fatigue.

As long as she can remember, this is who she has been. The one who fixes. The one who helps. She is a yes-girl. She believes that the opposite of control is confusion. She doesn't know yet that the opposite of control is faith.

She is busy, busy! She thinks this makes her a complete human. But sometimes it makes her half a human—a partial zombie wearing cuffed jeans and fair-trade earrings. She hopes this disguise will hide the chaos you don't see.

She'll tell you in a soothing tone that she's got it all under control. But to be honest, life feels out of control. And the more out of control it all gets, the more she wants to control it.

She tries to unwind—throwing a Lush bath bomb in the tub and sinking in—but this rest is an illusion. Inwardly, she is still managing, formulating, anticipating.

Yes. She is beginning to sense the spiral here. Yet she knows that some things can't be opted out of. She can't simply fire her life.

But—and this is really important—let's see her for who she really is. She loves fiercely. She is trying to hold it all together—*not* primarily because of her affinity for an ordered life, but because she loves deeply. Really, really deeply. She is an earnest defender of her family, her neighbors, the homeless guy on the corner, the starving child on the other side of the world. She pours out her life, like an offering, because she loves Jesus.

Yet she feels distant from all of them. She has gotten so busy caring, working, serving, and doing that she can't hear God's voice anymore.

She has lived by fear, instead of by faith.

She worries about things more than she prays about them.

She wants to let go, and she doesn't.

Can someone show her where to start? This is her life. She wants to live it.

She is me.

And maybe she is you too.

1

Invitation

The Help Your Weary Soul Longs For

ᴧᴧᴧᴧ

IF YOU ASKED ME five years ago, I naively would have told you that I didn't struggle with control. I would have said that I was a fully surrendered disciple of Christ. I mean, seriously—as long as everything went exactly the way I wanted it to, I was totally flexible.

I didn't intend to manipulate God by engaging in the most futile act known to humankind: trying to control one's life trajectory. And it's not that I *wanted* to control other people either. (Okay, so I might have been that take-charge kid in your high school class who led all the group projects and told you what to do—then resented everyone for not pulling their weight.)

Mostly, I wanted to control *myself*. If I ever had high expectations of anyone, it was of me. I wanted to present the self-assured, together version of my whole being. Which means I craved control over my face, my emotions, my body, my food, my words, my house, my schedule, my yard, my future.

My preference was a tidy, predictable, safe life where no one got hurt, where my kids remained in one piece, where there was no pain for anyone ever again, amen. My appetite for painlessness had me constantly minding the store. I hung on tight, so I could get life right.

Yet those old systems of coping weren't working.

Not long after I hit forty, I couldn't shake the truth that something needed to change. My desire to obsessively orchestrate what happened next was burning me out.

I ran out of gas.

Maybe the empty tank was God's way of bringing me to a dead stop, so I would finally pay attention. It worked. God got my attention, and maybe he's trying to get yours too.

Imagine that it's you who's run out of gas. Maybe that doesn't take much imagining after all, because like me, you're tired of trying to hold it together. You want to keep it all under control, but things aren't working out the way you planned.

If that sounds like you, picture it unfolding like this:

You're at the wheel, driving on fumes, pushing hard to get where you need to go because everyone is counting on you. The needle drops below *E*, and your car sputters to a stop, out of gas, at the edge of a dirt road. You are miles from where you want to be.

You rest your head on the steering wheel. It was only a matter of time. Here you are now. Empty.

But you are not alone.

Along comes a man, walking down the road toward you. The closer he gets, the more familiar he seems—the warm expression on his face, the worn hands, the creases around his eyes. You roll down the window, and he gives you an invitation, rolled up like a scroll. He waits, hands on his hips, smiling, because he's finally got your attention.

The hand-lettering reads: "You are cordially invited to embrace a new way of living. Help is here."

Sitting at the wheel, you feel your heart beat fast, as if a geyser has erupted inside your chest. You rarely ask for help, though let's be honest, you've needed help for a long time.

The man's eyes twinkle when he tells you that he can help you slow your frenetic pace to discover the life you were actually made for—a life of meaning, depth, and purpose.

Who wouldn't want this?

Your soul begs you to say yes. Because everywhere you go these days, you're pushing too hard. You're always in a hurry, eyes straight ahead, missing all the scenery. You arrive everywhere exhausted, with the tank near empty. Remember the days when you used to run your race feeling like a million bucks? You were driven and energetic; you made things happen. You were on your game, and nobody could stop you. You ran your race well, didn't you, girl? But lately, you feel like you're dragging a one-hundred-pound sack of bowling balls with you.

What if this invitation offers a way to travel lighter and be who you were meant to be, deep down?

You want to say yes, but you're scared of what this might cost you. Because you are the girl who is laser focused and responsible. You are never needy. So many people count on you. If you say yes to the invitation, what will you have to say *no* to? Whom will you disappoint? If you let go of everything you're holding on to, what might break? This all feels new and out of control, an unsteady, shifting place for a woman who has managed to make everyone believe she's got it "all under control."

The invitation is beautiful—but it isn't safe.

The man at the window is Jesus. You knew that.

Look, he won't force you to leap into the life you were made for, but he will shamelessly entice you. *Come*, he says. *I want to help.*

This is your invitation, the help your weary soul longs for. Will you say yes?

The Relentless Ways of Jesus

I said yes.

I would have been crazy not to—and you can't convince me otherwise, now that I know what I know.

But I didn't know any of that at first.

I'm the mom who habitually runs our Ford Explorer's gas

tank ridiculously close to empty. My record low on the digital gas gauge is an impressive two miles to empty.

I have managed my life the same way, running on fumes.

When I finally ran out of gas in my life, I saw Jesus coming down the dirt road.

He had been relentless for years, let me tell you. He delivered his invitation during a dozen Bible studies, countless nights of bed-tossing uneasiness, and those sermons that suddenly had me sitting up straight in my pew, like I'd been caught in the act.

I should have RSVP'd way back when, but I kept pushing, kept trying to hold it all together.

My condition: control.

Jesus spent years trying to tame my rather robust inner control freak. That side of me emerges at the mileposts of life, and also in the everyday moments: when team members in a project don't fulfill their obligations, when parked cars take up two spaces in the Target lot, when an airline pilot's youthful appearance leaves me with the sudden urge to research his credentials. Just last week, my inner control freak was triggered at the outdoor water park, where a whole army of shrieking kids were bobbing around in too-deep water as their Coppertone-slathered mothers worked on their tans. Like every other mom, I had come to the pool for fun, with a short stack of books and a foldable chair. But I couldn't find my chill anywhere. I was suddenly responsible for all the kids, and all the water, and all the possible pee in the pool. I had appointed myself chief of all the diving boards, all the slippery walkways, and all the sunscreen application. *It's all up to ME!* Everyone's life is *in my hands!*

So, yes, even there, Jesus encountered me, striding up sandal-footed next to my leopard-print flip-flops. He delivered that hand-lettered invitation poolside, a way of saying, "It's not all up to you, baby."

Oh, the indefatigable ways of Jesus. He slipped the invitation under the office door and under the pillow, between the pages of my too-full calendar and into my dream life, where my subconscious self always seems to be the first to know that I've stretched myself too thin, even as the rest of me fakes some semblance of fine. You know the kind of dream I'm talking about. It's the one in which you show up to college graduation, and only then do you remember that you forgot to attend all the required classes.

The invitations kept coming, and it was always my choice whether to RSVP.

I didn't say yes at first because of my vigorous control freakery. I didn't know what to do with that kind of invitation.

Here's why:

I like to gather up all the parts of my life into a neat pile, strategize exactly how they should turn out, and then ask God to bless my plans.

If I said yes to the invitation, what would it actually look like to let God take control? After all, I couldn't simply hand God my life and walk away while Jesus folded my husband's underwear and took all my calls.

So much of life clearly can't be opted out of. People

depend on me. I have kids to feed. A house to manage. Books to write. Committees on which to serve.

Most people can't simply fire their lives and move on when it all gets too chaotic. We need something more tangible than a slick phrase like "Just give it over to the Lord." Jesus calls us to something more sacrificial than running from responsibility. Following Jesus takes real *work*. Raising kids takes actual *effort*. We can't stop managing a household, cancel all our appointments, and spend the rest of our days on a floatie in the middle of a lake.

There are parts of my life where I don't get to throw my hands in the air and say, "I quit, God! This is all on you!" Believe me, there are times I *want* to. There are areas where I *do* want to channel my inner Elsa and "let it go." There are times I want to give it *all* to him—a complete handover—and spend the rest of the year hiding under the covers while eating entire bags of BoomChickaPop kettle corn.

But Jesus shows up at the foot of the bed and says, "Come on out, girl. You can do this. I am with you. Do. Not. Give. Up."

Recurring Nightmares of Control Freaks

- ▶ Showing up for the final exam—only to realize that you never attended any of the classes
- ▶ Losing all your sticky notes
- ▶ Realizing all the hand sanitizer is gone
- ▶ Being assigned to a group project at work and realizing that an inept person was picked as the leader
- ▶ Mixing up your kid's class picture day with crazy hair day
- ▶ Driving an out-of-control vehicle where the steering or brakes don't work
- ▶ Being called on in class, even though you haven't raised your hand
- ▶ Accidentally sending a series of romantic texts to your father-in-law

Spiritual surrender is more complex than any Christian platitude. And it's far more uncomfortable. I knew that if I said yes to his invitation, this partnership with Jesus would ask something of me. It would ask for *all* of me.

It will ask for all of you too.

The Comfort of Control

Confession: I have loved the steady comfort of control—even though it was only an illusion.

Control had become a coping mechanism to numb myself from the pain of life. I believed that even if I couldn't control the big things, I could at least *try* to control the little stuff: what I put in my mouth, how many steps I tallied on my Fitbit, my gray hairs, the vacuum lines in the carpet, how I scheduled every minute of every day, what you thought about me when I talked with you.

This has made me very busy, of course, and probably fairly annoying.

I've generally been able to handle a lot of tasks at once, and I've always been an achiever who won't easily back down from a challenge. Hard work has never scared me. But I can't begin to tell you how much my inner achiever propels me into dangerously high gear. I can't begin to tell you how I willingly withstand the mental pressure of believing I have to be "in control," reliable, on top of *all the things*—and how often that self-pressure completely breaks me. I've learned to hide the fractured debris of my overworked life. You will rarely find me confessing my anxiety. Why? Because that would make me appear too needy. You will never see me posting about it on Facebook with one of those cryptic messages: "Unspoken prayer request." Sadly, for a long time I didn't even ask my closest friends for prayer. I wouldn't have told them about the times my stress was so high that I would tremble and feel unable to breathe.

I kept saying I was fine.

But I wasn't fine.

I wanted help but didn't know how to ask for it. I said I trusted God but had reached the point where I realized I actually didn't. As a Jesus girl, this shocked me.

I had built my image as the helper, not as the helped. My life looked like this: *Here, let me write you another blog post. Here, let me send you an encouraging text. Sure, I can donate to your cause. Sure, I'll fill the spot on the committee. Sure, I can speak at your event.*

I was generally good at all of those tasks, but every yes became another drain on the internal gas tank. I had made myself indispensable and needed, and when insistent people handed me more responsibility, I stuffed it in the trunk of the car and forged ahead on the journey because "it was all under control."

All of this doing and striving was supposed to bring me happiness. With great surprise, I realized that it wasn't working out that way at all. Trying to wrap my arms around everything and everyone felt like attempting to herd baby kittens.

I turned around to face my life and realized that the woman I'd become wasn't someone I wanted to be around.

My calendar was crowded, and my body felt drained, pressurized, and frayed. I felt so much guilt because no matter what I was doing, I thought I should be doing something else. No matter what I did, it never seemed enough.

I began to ask myself questions like:

If I'm doing so much for others, why do I feel so distant
from them?
If I'm so busy, why am I not more productive?
How can I begin to truly trust a God whom I cannot see?
What is surrender anyway?
When do I let go, and when do I hang on tighter than ever
before?
If I've always been capable in the past, why does life feel so
chaotic now?

The answers to those questions became the book that you're holding in your hands.

I realized that I, the woman who had it "all under control," wasn't in control after all.

At last, I said yes to Jesus.

I accepted his frightening, exquisite, life-altering, outrageous invitation.

This book is my yes. I am writing every word of this book as if I were sitting next to you, at the side of a road, with your own gas-gauge needle on *E*.

Jesus is with us. He's handing you the same invitation that

he gave me: "You are cordially invited to embrace a new way of living. Help is here."

Strip Off Every Weight

I'm not the only one who needs help.

I know I'm not the only one because I've heard your pain. I've cried with you. I've read your e-mails in my in-box. I've watched you burn brightly, then flame out because you took on way too much. I see how you never say no because you can't handle the idea of disappointing anyone.

Underneath all of that "fine," you are in emotional pain. These are the sources of your distress:

- ► Some of your pain came because of all the things you're trying to *do*. You are tired.
- ► Some of your pain came because of all the things that happened *to* you. You are broken.

I saw life knock you down when you thought it was all under control. I attended your son's funeral. I cried with you after you found out about the affair. I held your hand after the miscarriage. I sat with you after you got the diagnosis. I drove you to your first appointment with your counselor.

This is who we are: We are women who are trying. Trying to hold it together for the sake of the family. Trying to give our best to our churches and jobs. Trying to be there emotionally and physically for the people we love. Trying to help our grown-up kids make good choices and then trying not to feel hurt when they tell us, "You're not helping, Mom; you're meddling."

I'm not the only one, and friend, you're not the only one either. So many things blindside all of us every day, and we can't control any of it.

The weather. Delayed flights. Our health. That awful text message. The traffic. The paths our kids choose. Our fertility—or lack thereof.

We ask for a map to deal with all of this, but instead Jesus gives us a compass and says, "Follow me."

Without a well-marked map, we try to draw our own. We execute plans to control this out-of-control life because we fear what will happen if we don't.

Along comes the invitation.

I have important news about this offer. It won't ask you to be someone you're not. It doesn't come with some unrealistic demand that you are suddenly going to stop being the incredibly brave and brilliant woman that you are. This invitation appreciates God's remarkable design in you. You're the capable kind of woman who reaches for the stars and gets things done. Do you know what a wonder you are?

You don't settle. You are the sort of woman we can count on to meet a work deadline, organize a food drive, take in the neighbors' kids during an emergency, drive your coworker to chemo, counsel a friend at 3 a.m. by text message, keep track of everyone's appointments, and make sure we're all wearing seat belts before you drive us on the three-day adventure that you single-handedly arranged. You're the one standing next

We ask for a map,
but instead
Jesus gives us a
compass and says,
"Follow me."

to me at the pool, ready to rescue any swimmer in distress. Solidarity, my friend.

We need you. We need capable, take-charge, charitable women like you as doctors and nurses in operating rooms where details like "proper disinfectant" matter. Let me tell it to you straight: If you have an inner control freak, I'm hoping you'll let her bust loose like nobody's business if someone I love is on your operating table. We need responsible women like you to *control all the bleeding*.

We also need you in charge of schools, nonprofits, and Fortune 500 companies. We need rock-star women like you to show us that surrender isn't "lie down in a pile." It's "march forward like a warrior." Sometimes surrendering to God will require you to do the hardest work you've ever done in your life: take in another foster child, fight for your marriage, kick cancer where the sun don't shine, or refuse to capitulate to the persistent drubbing from Satan.

Girl, listen up. We count on you. You are a woman fervently devoted to God's calling on your life, not only in your work but also in your relationships.

We need you because—let's face it: You save our behinds all the time. You are glue, holding your tribe together. Also? Your life reveals the source of true power: the Holy Spirit.

When you are at your best, you are plugged into the limitless resurrection power of God, who pulses through you with tremendous force. God created you for great things, and when you live as one empowered, you do those things really well. Standing ovation, sister!

But when you are under stress, you are probably like me: running dangerously close to empty a lot of the time. It's hard for you to tell the difference between what's essential and what's unimportant, so you do it all. You wrap your arms around everything, just in case. Without proper fuel, you try to generate your own strength—as if you can propel your car with your feet, like Fred and Wilma Flintstone. This leaves you worn out and calloused.

See if this resonates: *You need to get your control under control.* (Ask me how I know.)

Jesus is asking you and me to grab hold of this invitation so we can develop better habits and make choices that align with God's best for us. Saying yes to this invitation will teach us how to do things that, if we're honest with ourselves, we don't do well right now. Things like waiting, delegating, trusting an unseen God, being still, and yes . . . surrendering.

If you choose to accept this invitation, you can drive the route that's yours to drive, and drive it well, without the extra baggage and responsibility that you were never intended to carry.

Things My Girlfriends Said When I Told Them I Was Writing a Book on Control

- "I don't struggle with control. As long as everything goes according to plan, I'm super chill."
- "I'm not controlling, but can I show you the right way to write this book?"
- "Control isn't an issue for me. I just like having things go my way."
- "I don't need that book. I already know how to control everything."

Hebrews 12:1 gives us a clear picture of what this should look like:

> Let us strip off every weight that slows us down, especially the sin that so easily trips us up. And let us run with endurance the race God has set before us. (NLT)

It's like this: Let's say life is a car ride. A lot of us are carrying a little too much junk in the trunk, you know what I mean? We need to "strip off" that extra weight, as the writer of Hebrews tells us.

Stripping off extra weight looks a lot like surrender. You unload unnecessary baggage from the trunk and move forward with the *best*. You discard what isn't yours to carry so you can hang on to what *is*.

I'm right there with you. Let us strip off every weight that slows us down: our sin, our pride, our false sense of control, our need for approval, our badge of busyness, our belief that it's all in our hands. And then we can rise up with endurance to run the race God has set before us.

In our homes. In our churches. In our ministries. In our friendships. In whatever place he brings us—to a place of surrender.

What Surrender Actually Means

Here's what surrender is: Surrender is willfully accepting and yielding to God's plan for your life—no matter the cost.

When you live surrendered, you still have a job to do. There's nothing passive about surrender. Surrender isn't an act of weakness but of extraordinary strength that will propel each of us into the "race God has set before us." Don't think about surrendering control as giving up. Think of it as giving in to a greater power.

This is what's in store for us on this journey. Together we will:

- Stop playing God, and start becoming a partner with him in the life he's set before us.
- Let go of what God has *not* asked us to do, so we can shine at what he *has*.
- Learn that surrendered living is much more than "doing less." It's being more of who God created us to be.
- Rise up to do the incredible work of making better what God has put within our reach.
- Crack the "control code" so we can live with meaning and intention, rather than thinking we have to run the whole show.
- Stop burning bridges with people we love by giving them the freedom to live their lives without our constant supervision.
- Leave behind our frazzled lives and find a peace we almost forgot was possible.

If something doesn't change, our frenetic pace will become our new normal. We will continue banging our heads against the same brick wall, expecting something to change, while bleeding from the same old wounds.

My prayer is that every page of this book will whisper God's deep love for you, and that by the end, you'll be more peace-filled, more connected to God, and more present to the beautiful life you long for.

Perhaps you were hoping your guide would be someone who no longer struggles with issues of control, someone who consistently waits for God to act before leaping into action. Instead, you get me: a woman who is still learning how to let go of what *doesn't* matter, so she can build a life on what *does*.

In the pages ahead, you'll see that I rolled up my sleeves and asked God to help me redirect my misdirected paths. My favorite part is what happened when I lifted my whole life up to Jesus and said, "Here, can you help me untangle this?" Together, we're loosening the knots.

Can you imagine partnering with Jesus in this way? Jesus is still standing on that dirt road by your car, hands on his hips. I imagine him smirking a little because he finally got you to slow down enough to pay attention. Isn't he clever?

Up ahead, you see an old Honda.* Jesus wants you to leave that empty tank behind and climb inside his car.

Of course, as Carrie Underwood will sing to you, Jesus is definitely taking the wheel. But make no mistake: There are times when he's going to ask you to do some driving.

---

*Scholars seem to agree that Jesus drove a Honda, but he didn't talk about it publicly. "For I did not speak of my own Accord" (John 12:49, NIV). So there you have it: a Honda. I don't know exactly who first made this startling discovery, but I learned about it on the Internet, so it must be true.

Don't think of Jesus as your chauffeur; he is more like your driver's ed coach. He's there to teach you his rules of the road.

Friend, do not fear the wheel. You have been equipped to drive—and Jesus is beside you when you steer the wrong way. Hopefully he will pull the emergency brake if necessary, and I've personally put in a request for roads lined with padded walls.

The windows are rolled down, the music is cranked, the tank is full, and there's something that looks like freedom on the horizon. Today that's where I am—driving into freedom, with one hand on the wheel and the other hand shot high toward the sky.

Out on the open road, may you feel the reassuring love of Jesus. I think it's safe to say he's glad you said yes. On this journey, you'll discover that, at last, it really *is* all under control: God's.

Cracking the Control Code

You have likely invested a lot of time into your lists, your schedule, your retirement savings account, and your children's college fund. You have all kinds of ways to be efficient in your work. You are a master of many things. Now you get to apply those skills toward rearranging your life in a way that aligns your priorities with God's.

This will require a plan. That's why every chapter of this book offers you a way to take action by "cracking the control code."

What is the control code? It is the system of ideas, rules, and behaviors that we have set for ourselves to keep our lives in order. We want to crack that code so we can understand why we operate the way we do. Then we can replace those old systems with healthy living.

In order to crack the control code, each chapter invites you to consider new practices and new ways of thinking. This will require an investment of your time. It will take energy. Change does not happen automatically. This book is going to ask something of you as you move to another level in your spiritual maturity. To enhance this experience, consider obtaining the *It's All Under Control Bible Study: A 6-Week Guided Journey*.

Why all the work? Because you are not a grape; you do not mature just by existing.

We cannot function as if spiritual maturity is programmed into us. We would never operate that way in other areas of our lives. We would never leave our jobs to chance, our finances unplanned, our babies in anything less than a five-point harness car seat. But often, we have no strategy for the most important role of our lives: that of a disciple who truly trusts the Leader enough to follow where he's going.

Take heart: If anyone can do this, it is us. We are the women who aren't afraid of a challenge. Let's do this.

The First Step: Running Smarter

You have a race to run. But first you must strip off every weight that slows you down from running the course God has set out for you. Consider everything you feel responsible for at this time in your life—the good, the bad, the beautiful, the ugly, the hard, and the effortless. As you take an honest assessment of where you are now, consider your work, household duties, children, relationships, volunteer assignments, church commitments, personal struggles, and aging parents, for instance. Also consider other "weights" that you carry. Are there areas where you've said yes because you don't want to disappoint people? Are there weights you carry simply because you are trying to please people? Do you employ coping mechanisms—such as exercise, food, addictive substances—to give you a sense of control?

Now you're ready to begin creating your list. You can download a free printable journaling sheet designed specifically for this exercise from my website at www.ItsAllUnderControlBook .com/Resources, or you can make your own with the following instructions:

1. Write this Bible verse at the top of the page: "Let us strip off every weight that slows us down, especially the sin that so easily trips us up. And let us run with endurance the race God has set before us" (Hebrews 12:1, NLT).

2. Draw two columns. Label one column "My Race"; label the other "Junk in the Trunk."

3. As you consider every weight you identified, ask God to help you discern what you were meant to carry and what you weren't.

4. Under "My Race," list the items that you sense are yours to carry on this journey with Jesus. This list will likely include many things you love. It will also include items that feel especially heavy right now—responsibilities that you can't avoid or difficult circumstances that you are facing today, such as grief, that you must carry for a time.

5. Under "Junk in the Trunk," list items that you were never intended to carry. These are items that God may be calling you to "strip off" because they slow you down. This list may take longer to compile, and it will require ruthless honesty with yourself. The items on this list may include coping mechanisms, toxic relationships, approval-seeking behaviors, duties that are no longer yours to perform, and commitments that exhaust you.

6. Look over your two lists. As you do so, thank God for the race you're running. Praise him for the beautiful parts, and ask him to help you deal with the hard parts. Then seek his help in removing the junk in the trunk, bit by bit. This is where the real change begins.

Let us strip off every weight that slows us down. We have a race to run.

2

Illusion

The Reason We Are the Way We Are

∧∧∧∧∧

HOW DID I GET HERE?

That was my thought as I lay flat on my back in two feet of snow, out in the never-ending expanse of rural Iowa. I was caked in white one hundred yards from our house, staring up at the sky, domed above me in sheet-iron gray. A few stray flakes floated down, gently swinging like tiny feathers in the breeze. My daughters, near the front door, yelled across our farm fields: "Mom, are you all right?"

I was all right. But I was stuck.

I wiped the hair out of my eyes with a snow-covered glove and let all my breath out in one huge sigh, fogging up my glasses.

I was so, so stuck. And now I couldn't see.

On this December day, my mission involved venturing outside so I could retrieve hay from one of our tightly wound bales, all lined up in neat rows on the edge of the field. I'd read online how a mom could promote Christmas kindness in her home with a project involving hay. Every time her children performed an act of kindness during Advent, they could take a piece of hay and put it inside the nativity scene. On Christmas Day, Jesus' manger would be lined with kindness.

So right after lunch, I zipped up my parka as I peered out the front window. Just a few hours before, Snowpocalypse had finally blown over, harrumphing its bad self toward Illinois. It was one of the biggest blizzards we'd seen in ages. "Not to worry," I said to the girls as I flung a plaid wool scarf around my neck and headed out the door toward the field.

I had visions of me gliding gracefully across bucolic farm fields, like an Olympic medalist on skates. I forgot that I was a farmer's wife in heavy snow boots.

The drifts were deceptively deep. I lugged my feet along, as if I were dragging myself out of the unforgiving pull of quicksand. Mother Nature doesn't mess around up here, people.

All of a sudden, my sense of balance failed me, right when the hay bales were cruelly within reach. I toppled. One leg twisted itself out of the boot, and there I lay, sock-footed and helpless, with the strange wet burn of winter prickling my toes.

My girls had been watching the whole sorry saga unfold. After yelling across the field to check on my well-being, they did what any good Christian girls would do in response to their fallen and beloved mother: They laughed hysterically. Then they promised to rush to my aid. This took approximately forever.

Their slow rescue gave me plenty of time to ask myself the question: *How did I get here?*

There's a short answer. And there's a long answer.

The short answer is this: I want the idyllic Christmas—one that will be memorable years later for our children. This desire kicks in soon after Thanksgiving every year, when we begin decorating. I make hot cocoa, pop in my *Osmond Family Christmas* CD, and flip the fireplace switch on the wall. *Thwock!* Instant flames.

In our home, the season doesn't really begin until I make my annual proclamation, ensuring that *this* Christmas will capture the true meaning of the holiday.

On that particular year, before a single stocking was hung, I prayed that God would reorient my focus. I had seen on Facebook how other moms were preparing. So I bought an Advent wreath. I hid our two-inch resin Jesus because I read somewhere that the baby shouldn't appear in our nativity scene until Christmas Day. I told the girls about our big plans to truly celebrate Christmas the way God intended—because he is super-concerned about whether our mantels look like the ones on Pinterest.

The girls stood gape-mouthed.

"Isn't this what you said last year?" Anna asked.

The color drained from Lydia's cheeks when I spoke of a simpler Christmas with a renewed focus on Jesus.

"Does this mean we won't be getting presents?" she asked.

(Incidentally, a few days after the Snowpocalypse fiasco, I accidentally flushed my Mastercard down the toilet. I wondered: *Is this God's strange way of answering my prayer for a more focused Christmas?* By the way, standing in the bathroom doorway as the plumber fishes a credit card out of your toilet is a whole new level of embarrassing.)

Back to the story. I reassured the girls they'd still get presents, but we'd redouble our efforts to focus on Christ. I explained that I'd be going out to their dad's fields to get the needed hay for our manger project. And off I went.

That's where you find me now—bespectacled and sprawled in snow.

Even if it's summer wherever you are today, put on your snowsuit and lie beside me for a moment, friend. Join me here in the middle of my Iowa winter, where the scents of soggy mittens and evergreen trees mingle in the jagged, icy air. Because now comes the long answer to the question I asked at the beginning of this chapter:

How did I get here? How did we get here?

I'm guessing you've looked around at your life and asked yourself the same questions: *How did I get here? How did I get to this flat-on-my-back place where I am wiped out to the core? I feel like I'm doing all the right things, but on the inside, something feels off. I'm doing so much and succeeding at about 43 percent of it.*

Some might say we got here because we're control freaks who can't stand anything second-rate. (I think I just stepped on every one of my frostbitten toes there.)

But hold on. It's not that simple. There's a deeply complicated and sincere reason we find ourselves stuck in this place. We got here because we care. We got here because we desire lives of meaning and connection. Sometimes, out of love, we push ourselves far.

On that Christmas, my deepest desire was for my family to have a meaningful holiday with Jesus at center stage. I'd move heaven, earth, and a thousand snowdrifts to make it happen. My mishap was a harmless incident that still makes me laugh. But that same yearning—to care for others—is why I drive myself to the brink of insanity the other 364 days of the year. And it's no laughing matter.

My deep affection for my people is why I'm often thinking, managing, planning. I feel like it all depends on me. If I *do* hand anything completely over to God, I tend to come back daily to monitor his progress. My preference is to lift my perfectly strategized life up to Jesus and say, "This is how it's gonna be. Are we cool with that?"

And then I go about making it happen, out of love.

My children *will* be happy because out of love I'll create memorable experiences for them.

My church family *will* be happy because my love drives me to say yes to whatever is needed.

My friends *will* be happy because my love refuses to let them down.

Furthermore, I live under the false assumption that if I handle everything, I can shield my beloved people from pain.

I've believed that if I could get my arms around everything, no one would get hurt. If you're like me, you are the protector and the supervisor. A lot of times, you're trying to keep your people happy—and at the very least, *alive*.

This explains our ardent devotion to charts. (Exhibit A: I once kept a poop and pee chart. I tracked our newborns' excrement because I wanted to make sure I was properly hydrating the tiny humans. All in the name of love, people.)

I'm a total Marlin. Remember him? He's the fish-daddy whose highest priority was Nemo's well-being. "I promise I will never let anything happen to you, Nemo," Marlin said, cradling an egg that would soon become a clown fish. I can so relate. I want to inoculate my kids from pain and "help them succeed."

It's why I lie awake at night, planning my response to worst-case scenarios, operating as if my worldview is worry. I thought this sort of managed life would give me what I longed for: more peace, less fear; more meaning, less aimlessness; more love, less angst.

I want depth, but I stay stuck in the shallows—because I'm strung so thin. My desire to love well is why I say yes too often. It's why I overcommit, why I make extravagant plans to bring meaning to every holiday, why I plan for every possible outcome in every possible situation so I am fully prepared. It's also why I find myself flat on my back—again and again—with peace and joy far out of reach.

How did we get here?

We got here . . . because of love.

I started here, with love, because this is a shame-free zone. Let's dwell in love and grace for a minute, okay? Yes, far uglier reasons fuel controlling behaviors—fear, the desire to be right, a hunger for approval. (We will dig into those motivations throughout the book.) But we begin with love. So many of us feel like we've got to run the show, and we feel that way because we care. If we don't do it, who will?

Important distinction here: I'm not talking about the narcissistic controller who tries to dominate people and pass it off as "caring." I'm talking about women like you—who adore Jesus and are deeply moved by that love to make life beautiful. Your heart is precious and filled with the best motives.

But even for those of us with good intentions, our caring can cross over into behavior that makes us miserable, anxious, tired—and probably less pleasant to be around. We even find *ourselves* annoying.

That's how it goes down for me every so often when I'm in charge of worship music at our little country church. About once a month, I am assigned the task of selecting contemporary music from our iTunes library and projecting the lyrics onto big screens in the front. (I call myself the church DJ.)

But watch out when DJ Jenny Lee's in the House during that stressful fifteen minutes before worship starts. I know I have probably offended people who wanted to have a friendly chat with me at the back of church before the service began.

Instead of my kindness, they received my cold shoulder. Why? Because I was busy trying to create a meaningful and perfect worship experience for them—driven by my love for Jesus and every member of my church family. Ironically, the people I intended to serve wouldn't feel love if they stood within ten feet of me and my beloved iTunes library.

On some Sundays, we may be singing "O Come to the Altar," but I'd advise anyone entering the sanctuary to take the route to the altar that bypasses the agitated DJ!

I have regretted all the times that my well-meaning "acts of kindness" have made me as pleasant as a rabid porcupine. But where do I find the balance? How do I do the work I'm called to do without alienating the people I intended to love in the first place?

I think it starts by acknowledging that pride can masquerade as love. We think it's all on us. But it's *not* on us. It's on God. Pride says, "I know more than God what is good for my life and what is good for my people. Besides, I'm doing this out of love!"

God says, "Trust a love greater than your own. This does not depend on you. Instead, you must depend on me."

The Illusion We All Fall For

Let's go back to where it all started: the Garden of Eden. Eve didn't set out to mess everything up for all of humanity. I think she was like us—a woman with good intentions who, in this instance, made a very poor choice. She narrowed in on a piece of forbidden fruit because she thought it would bring more meaning to her life. She probably never imagined the cataclysmic results.

"When the woman saw that the fruit of the tree was good for food and pleasing to the eye, and also desirable for gaining wisdom, she took some and ate it" (Genesis 3:6).

Good intentions get the best of us, don't they?

Eve probably didn't go into her day with a diabolic item on her to-do list.

Prune roses. *Check.*

Feed the goofy-looking animals with really long necks. *Check.*

Take stroll with God around lake. *Check.*

Try out new fruit. *Check.*

Usher sin into world. *Check.*

Neither do we go into our days thinking, *I'm going to be a control freak today and make myself miserable.* Instead, we go into our days with self-made edicts of love. No one is more surprised than us when we turn around and find ourselves plucking forbidden fruit from trees that we had no business touching.

There's a fine line between unhealthy

Famous Bible Characters with Control-Freak Tendencies

▶ Jonah—He didn't want to go where God called him to go, so he hitched a ride on a boat. On a positive note, he was the first human in recorded history to become fish bait—and live to tell about it.

▶ Saul—This impulsive king had a hard time letting God be God and often did things he was never asked to do.

▶ Sarai—God promised her a child. When she couldn't get pregnant, she took matters into her own hands, suggesting her husband sleep with one of the servants. Who could have predicted *that* wouldn't work?

▶ Martha—Okay. You knew she'd be on the list. But can we just stand in solidarity with Martha for a moment? We would have been right in that kitchen with her. How else are people supposed to eat?

control and healthy control, and that line is drawn with the pen of good intentions.

At our best, those good intentions produce meaning and joy. Your good intentions are why you are famous for always managing to find the perfect Christmas gift for everyone on your list. You are the cool mom who sends the best snacks to preschool. But at your worst, your own good intentions can leave you all angsty, with zero chill. Sometimes you might even end up alienating people you cherish.

For instance, I have a friend whose mom used to visit her from out of state. Invariably, one of the first things this mother would do was clean out and rearrange my friend's pantry. It was an act of love on the mother's part, but it drove my friend crazy because her mom never asked if she wanted her to do it. (She didn't.)

Ultimately, Eve's decision to take the fruit was about control. She wanted to be like God. It can be painful to admit that we sometimes want the same thing. But—*oh, this is hard to say*—sometimes we act as if we know more than God about what's good for us—or for our loved ones and their messy pantries.

I'm not excusing our behavior, but we need to know this: Our desire for control doesn't make us freaks; it makes us human. Science reveals an interesting truth about control. We all have an inner appetite for it.

For instance, people believe they are less likely to get in a car accident if they are in high-control situations, such as when they are driving. They feel more vulnerable in low-control situations, such as when they are sitting in the passenger seat. Another study showed that people are more likely to believe they'll win the lottery if they pick their own numbers.[1]

In short, people tend to feed themselves the delusion that *I'm safer and more secure if I'm in charge.* Holley Gerth, a best-selling author and certified life coach, said this:

> We go through life afraid of a lot of different things, and we think "If I can just have complete control, then I would be safe." We may not even articulate that to ourselves but that's what we really want is to be safe. So when we want control, suddenly we're responsible for everything and everyone. And that is a very stressful way to live. . . . And it's all an illusion anyway, because we don't have control.[2]

The desire for control—even the illusion of it—powerfully seduces.

Long ago, sin seeded the human psyche with the idea that it needed to get its fingers into everything. Furthermore, our human psyche bought into the notion that if we *didn't* have control, we were failing. That feeling is compounded by our dominant cultural narratives. Look to the ads for proof. No matter what seems out of control, there's something you can buy or do to get it "all under control." Botox. A new diet plan. A different closet organizational system. Dandruff shampoo. Another self-help book. Spanx.

I can look back and identify where I've wanted to be the boss of my whole life. Control started at age three: "I do it myself, Mommy!" At age sixteen, Noxzema. At age twenty-three, control-top panty hose. At age thirty-three, a pile of self-help books. At age forty-three, a hair-color appointment every few months.

Wanting control is an inborn trait that's hard to shake.

When we began to follow Jesus, we relinquished that control. But we constantly try to steal it back because we think we'll be safer if we're in control. Years ago, I would have told you that I trusted Jesus, but honestly, it was difficult for me to entrust my cares to someone I couldn't actually *see*.

And then, *boom*. A car accident on an icy Iowa highway jolted me back into my ultimate spiritual reality—that I don't have as much control as I thought.

It was 2009. Another car crossed the center line, slamming into my Toyota van. The accident was an absolute "Jesus take the wheel" moment in my life, as the power steering went out. The van spun, the windows shattered, and I had no say in any of it. My life was wholly in God's hands. God alone would determine whether I would see my daughters and husband again. It was one of the most vulnerable moments of my life—granting me an acute awareness of milliseconds, of my own breath, of the fragility of life, of God's complete control and my lack thereof.

In that moment, I gave up control that I never really had in the first place. My hands literally and figuratively came off the wheel as my car spun and landed in a snow-packed ditch.

One day after the accident, back at home, I made a renewed commitment to let Jesus take total control of my life—a job that was already actually *his*. There was this moment I'll never forget, and in fact, my husband memorialized it with a photo on his flip phone. I'm sitting in the recliner with both girls on my lap and a set of crutches on the floor. Lydia was eight years old. She kept telling me, "You smell like hospital," and Anna, age five, looked at me like I was a mystery to be solved. The image is too grainy to see the tears in my eyes, but they were there. That afternoon, I kept glancing at our daughters through tear-blurred vision, and then toward my husband, and then out the windows overlooking our vast fields, twinkling with snow as if God had studded our corner of the world with diamonds.

"This is all yours, God," I told him. "And I am all yours. Thank you for my life."

I thought the accident had cured me of trying to be the CEO of everything.

But then life happened. Days turned into months, and months into years. I became the old me. The apostle Paul must have known how I felt: "I don't really understand myself, for I want to do what is right, but I don't do it. Instead, I do what I hate" (Romans 7:15, NLT).

Perhaps you have had lightbulb moments like I had—a brush with death, a Sunday message you swear was preached just for you, a divine appointment in an unexpected place. You make your oaths, but in time, you slide away from full surrender and regress into your former school-superintendent self.

Here's what my regression looked like: I *again* became a self-reliant woman who would go to Google before God; who would try to manage outcomes; who would hustle and strive and take matters into my own hands. It's the American way, baby—value individualism, do whatever you set your mind to.

We've become so scarily self-sufficient—even as Christians. We believe in God, but we don't actually rely on him. We manage our lives instead of living them. We pray, "Give us this day our daily bread," but if we run out of bread, we drive the Escalade to Costco to buy in bulk what we don't really need anyway.

We're a society of problem solvers and outcome managers. We don't merely raise our kids; we control who they will become. We're more than helicopter parents; we're lawn mower parents. Instead of "hovering" like helicopters over our kids' lives, we go one step further—clearing the preferred path for our children.[3]

Here's the crazy truth: In a world that feels like it's gone out of control, we actually *have* more control than ever. Mobile devices to track our kids' locations, our heart rates, our bank accounts. Pain management for whatever hurts. TSA agents to keep airports safe. Yet, with all that control, Americans are among the most anxious people in the world.[4]

If we've got it all under control, why are we so wrecked and weary?

"I Am Not the Christ"

So often, I have treated God as an employee instead of CEO of my life. If I truly let him lead, I was afraid of what would happen. If I surrendered my marriage to him, would it survive? If I gave him my children, would they be okay? If I left my finances in his hands, would the bills get paid?

More than two thousand years ago, John the Baptist showed us what it looks like to let God be God. John the Baptist was the one appointed by God as a messenger to announce the arrival of Jesus. Priests and Levites kept asking questions like, "Who's the dude with the weird diet and strange clothes?" John cut right to the chase and set the record straight. He let everyone know who he *was* by first telling them who he *wasn't*: "I am not the Christ" (John 1:20, ESV).

I want that to be true in my life—that I would let Christ be Christ. I am not the Christ! I didn't cross-check with the Greek or anything, but I'm pretty sure God isn't taking applications for his position.

Repeat after me: "I am not the Christ."

When we stop trying to *be* Jesus, the astonishing result is that we actually become more *like* him. We begin to hear him speak more clearly. We gain clearer vision of the direction he has for us. We make better decisions. And ultimately, we love the way he loves, which was our motivation all along.

How did we get here?

We got here because of love. And that's also how we're going to get out of this flat-on-our-back place. With love.

When we stop
trying to be Jesus, the
astonishing result is
that we actually become
more like him.

But it's not all on us. We are going to get out of this place by the *power of God's love that compels us.* I believe it deep within me: In the firm grasp of Jesus' hands, we will not be constrained. His grip is going to set us free.

About That Christmas I Got Stuck

You may be wondering: Did I ever find the true meaning of Christmas, as I so desperately wanted when I got stuck in the snow?

Weeks passed, and Christmas Eve came. Behold: The fake fireplace was ablaze with gas-fueled, synthetic flame. The Osmond CD circled itself around the player for the 160th time of the season. As I pulled another dozen cookies out of the oven, Anna came into the kitchen before bedtime.

"Mom?" she said. "I think you should put some hay in the manger."

"Because of the cookies?" I asked, pleased that she'd noticed my act of kindness.

"No, Mom," she said. "Because you love us and you help us know about Jesus."

Man, as much as I'm messing stuff up some days, there are other days when I'm getting it right. I need to hold on to those moments.

I tucked her into bed, turned out the lights, and after everyone was in bed, I put a piece of hay in the manger scene. It felt right this time. I stood there awhile in the glow of moonlight that shone through the window, pooling on our little nativity. I thought about what I'd learned that year:

Some days, my love for my people will have me flat on my back. Some days, I'll get it all wrong. But some days, I will get it right.

And you will too. Remember that thing that motivates you? It's love. Hold tight to it. It will serve you well.

As we move along on this journey, we will have more right days than wrong days. I'm sure of it. And yeah. We're still going to do ridiculous things in the name of love.

Before I went to bed that night, I vowed to let go a little more each day. I asked God to place within my hands what he intended for me to hold all along. And I asked him to restrain me from constantly monitoring what was solely his to handle.

Holiday Moments That Bring Out the Worst in Us

- You rented extra chairs for the living room, but guests insist on lingering in your small kitchen.

- Your kids insist on helping you decorate the tree but do not appreciate symmetry.

- Your husband swipes cheese from the tray before everyone arrives, completely messing up your straight rows.

- Your mother-in-law surpasses the spending limit for the kids—by a lot.

- You planned for thirty people. Fifty show up.

- Kids arrive at your door for Halloween in jeans and a sweatshirt. And they actually expect candy from you.

- You finish your Christmas shopping in July—and then forget where you hid all the gifts.

- During "Silent Night" at the midnight Christmas Eve service, everyone else enjoys a holy moment with lit candles, while you scan for the nearest fire exits—just in case.

- Your family decides to take a holiday road trip. It turns out that your family's interpretation of "We're leaving at 6 a.m." is *not* the same as *your* interpretation of "We're leaving at 6 a.m."

(I made two more vows that night: To never play outside in post-blizzard hours, and to keep my credit card in my purse instead of my back pocket.)

I did find the meaning of Christmas that year. I found it in the carols, the spritz cookies, the light snowfall outside the window. I found it when our family gathered on the couch with all of our hands reaching into one big bowl of popcorn while watching *Elf*. I found it in the girls' squeals of delight when they opened their American Girl dolls. I even found it in that cheesy activity where we lined Jesus' manger with hay.

But mostly, I found it in the story: "Today in the town of David a Savior has been born to you; he is the Messiah, the Lord" (Luke 2:11).

The story of Jesus coming down to earth is a beautiful picture of what it means to let go and give this life your all—all in the name of love.

Thank you, Jesus.

Cracking the Control Code 〰〰〰〰〰〰〰〰

1. **Control Code Continuum.** I have created a continuum to help you figure out when you've moved from healthy to unhealthy patterns of behavior. What's a continuum, you ask? You know those charts in hospital rooms, where you have to describe your pain level based on the smiley-face scale? That's a continuum.

   Review the Control Code Continuum on page 255 and then return to it regularly, because it will help you determine what you can do to operate within the "Healthy Zone."

   You can also find the continuum online at www.ItsAll UnderControlBook.com/Resources.

2. **"I am not the Christ."** Ask God to bring to mind times in your life when you've had good motives that ended with bad results, like I did that Christmas. Consider times when you've tried to take over a child's school project, resolve a conflict on someone else's behalf, "fix" your spouse, or create a memorable experience, only to have it stress you out (along with everyone else).

   In your journal or on a piece of paper, write down a word or phrase that represents those times in your life. Behind each one of them, write, "I am not the Christ."

3

Awesome

When Being "In Control" Gets Out of Control

∧∧∧∧

THE MAMMOGRAM ROOM. The one place on earth where I feel utterly out of control and, well . . . exposed. If you haven't had one yet, don't worry; it's not so bad. It's about as pleasant as you would imagine. For the uninitiated, try this to get a similar effect: Strip down in kitchen, open refrigerator door, insert one breast, allow strange woman to slam door on it, hold your breath, die a little inside. Switch sides. Repeat.

I got my yearly mammogram last month, and as usual, a familiar fidgety anxiety rose up in me. It's not the procedure itself that bothers me the most. It's the callback.

Every year, a nurse recommends that I return to the office for follow-up testing because my breast tissue is very dense, which makes tumor detection difficult. (I'm a little emotional over the fact that you and I have already become so close that, by chapter 3, we can talk openly about breast density.)

Last month, I got another callback and returned for a follow-up ultrasound. The ultrasounds are typically lengthy because my breasts are not only dense but scattered with cysts. Those cysts, on first glance, can look like tumors. As you can imagine, the ultrasound appointment is pretty stressful until they check everything out and give me the all clear.

At my recent appointment, the ultrasound technician remarked about my cystic, tangled breast tissue: "My, my," she said, waving an ultrasound wand at the screen, "you have very busy breasts."

Yep. Busy breasts. It's a thing.

Go figure: Even my boobs are busy.

The High Cost of Being Awesome

I've always been a busy girl.

Maybe you can relate. People ask you how you've been, and more often than not, your answer is "busy." You are busy from head to foot—and in my case, a couple of places in between. Busyness is the natural by-product of a responsible woman like you, whom others depend on. You never intended to hop on the hamster wheel, but once you find yourself spinning, you aren't sure how to get off.

I am fascinated by Ann Burnett's research on the impact of fast-paced lifestyles. Burnett, a professor at North Dakota State University, told an interviewer how she'd been asked to speak at a conference on the "pace of life." The invitation came a few weeks before Christmas, and as she was pondering the topic, the flood of holiday cards arrived in her mailbox. In every card, "people talked about how they were busy, how their kids were busy, how they were so busy last year they hadn't even written a letter. Everyone was busy, from the five-year-old to the retiree."[1]

Turns out, the holiday letters of your own pastor, priest, or youth leader might not be so different. Ministry leaders are often overcommitted yet feel powerless to say no. Here's the irony: Christian leaders are called to shepherd others into a place of rest—yet they rarely give themselves permission to do the same. Even if you're not in a ministry leadership position, chances are you feel busy. In a survey, 752 Christian leaders were asked to respond to this statement: "The busyness of my life gets in the way of developing my relationship with God." Seventy-five percent of those surveyed responded that this is "often" or "almost always" true of them.[2]

That's a strikingly high percentage, especially for a group of people who follow the Prince of Peace and the author of rest.

For better or worse, I've always described myself as a busy person. When I was twenty-two, I left our family Christmas early to write obituaries for the newspaper. I was a college news intern for the *Des Moines Register*, and my editor needed me to report to the obit desk by noon.

My parents stood beside our twinkling flocked tree and waved from the living room window as I pulled out of the driveway, snow crunching under the tires of my Geo Storm. They were sad to see me leave on a holiday, of course, but more than their disappointment, I sensed their pride. Perhaps they saw the fruit of their parenting. They'd success-fully molded me into a young woman with a strong work ethic and a deep sense of responsibility.

Hard work runs in our family. My dad was the CEO of a grain-elevator company, the son and grandson of farmers. Mom didn't have a fancy job title, but as a stay-at-home mother, she was one of the hardest workers I knew—an ethic learned in the barns with her father in the 1940s and 1950s. As an adult, she somehow managed to keep a spotless home while raising four kids, singing in a traveling trio, and volun-teering in our community.

All of my siblings grew up to hold high-level jobs in administration or sales, and they married similarly minded people. My younger brother is one of the top-selling casket salesmen in the country, but it wasn't enough for him to know the hardware of a casket. He wanted to understand the science and care of the body, so he got a degree in mortuary science.

Like my casket-selling brother, I was keenly aware that death didn't take holidays. That meant the newsroom needed someone to work the obit desk on Christmas Day. When asked, I said yes. Maybe it's that I hadn't learned yet how to say no. Maybe I harbored fears of disappointing someone. Maybe I simply remembered the truth: *I was the intern.*

I obediently sat at my desk, away from my relatives, who,

under the trance of a turkey dinner, watched through half-closed lids as George Bailey learned the meaning of life in his hometown of Bedford Falls. Yet I don't remember feeling a sense of regret or loss. I do remember the editor meeting me at the entrance of the newsroom, telling me how "awesome" it was that I took the holiday shift. I remember how awesome it made me feel too.

All in all, I'm grateful for a genetic disposition toward productivity and dependability. I'm generally able to juggle many tasks at once, and if you ask me to do something, it's as good as done. Few things in life give me greater joy than knowing my work has made someone's life better or happier. That value system chiefly drove my work as a reporter. But that same desire resulted in long workdays because I did not know what the word *moderation* meant. You know the saying: "If you want something done, ask a busy woman to do it." People kept asking, and I responded with an almost unstoppable series of yeses.

I left the newsroom in my midthirties. But even when I became a work-at-home mom, I was a high-functioning multitasker, consulting with a book editor by phone while sorting laundry with my feet instead of my hands because I was cradling the child who just puked on me.

My high tolerance for heavy workloads still makes me feel pretty awesome because I can usually look back on a day and find something I accomplished. Maybe you're the same way. At the end of the day, you review your list and see all the neat X's in all the square boxes, and you feel awesome.

Until you don't.

You can handle a lot of tasks at once, until you can't.

You *do*, *do*, *do*, and say yes to one more thing—thinking you can handle it all, remembering the buzz you get from productivity.

When I turned forty, I began looking around at my life in a more reflective way. I noticed two dark half-moon circles under my eyes, staring back at me in the mirror. There was the slumped posture, the yawn at dinner, the numbness, the realization that I'd gone too far. Again.

And so I pledged to slow down. But in time I wound my way back to busy again.

Sound familiar?

This is the high cost of being awesome.

Think of yourself as a kitchen pantry in a brand-new house. When we designed our home among the cornfields, we had the builder draw a large pantry in the plan—a place to store canned goods, cookbooks, and small appliances. When we moved in, I had so much room in the pantry that I could literally space cans in neat rows, three inches apart. Within a year, I couldn't find room for a single box of Cheerios in the same pantry. So I'd hastily take a few items out—stale crackers, expired canned goods. But soon more stuff would crowd in, forcing me to again return to the pantry with a garbage sack.

That's how it can get with life: You reach fever pitch, and there's no room for anything else. You scan the shelves of your life and hastily toss a few items—you know, quit a committee and turn down an invitation to join a second book group. You pledge to do better from here on out, brush your hands together, and then move on.

But invariably, you crave the buzz of productivity. An interior urge compels you to fill the shelves again. Your agenda enslaves you again. The pattern repeats itself every few months, and you get the feeling that you've never really gotten it right.

For my part, I thought this lifelong problem would rectify itself when we moved to the farm from the city. The relocation greatly decreased my work responsibilities—I kept my job at the paper but worked part-time, writing only a handful of stories every week from my office on the farm.

But like I'd always done, I filled the shelves of my life—this time with new things, as if I'd discovered a shiny new supermarket aisle from which to shop and fill the pantry. I became a tremendously busy worker for Jesus. I started a blog, taught journalism at a nearby Christian college, led the town's vacation Bible school program, and later began writing books and speaking across the United States. Meanwhile, I was the mom of two girls, the wife of a farmer, and the co-keeper of a small herd of cats.

Seeing it all written out like that, my life was a Jenga tower, one wooden block away from toppling.

My willingness to be "in control" of a lot of things often got out of control. Of course, I'd tell you I had it under control. But in rare moments of honesty with myself, I knew I didn't. I stacked the pantry shelves, so to speak, until there was no room.

So much of this stacking was about proving myself to someone. In news, I tried to prove myself to editors, stretching my arms toward "awesome." I'm going to tell it to you straight. After a few years in ministry, I could see a new problem developing: I had begun trying to prove myself to God. I wanted to be awesome for Jesus.

Somewhere between the newsroom and the farm, my heart for Jesus grew so big. If you read anything I wrote during that season, you were never going to miss how much I loved Jesus. If you read my Facebook posts, you'd know how much I loved Jesus. If you listened to my keynote addresses at conferences, you'd know how much I loved Jesus. If you heard my private prayers with our daughters, you'd know how much I loved Jesus.

God knows I loved him big back then, a love that has continued to grow to this day. There have been barren and parched seasons with Jesus, but quite often it's been intense and fiery. I've wanted him to know how much I loved him. How he was the reason for everything.

But Jesus exposed a flaw in my thinking when he stepped into the pantry that is my life. He looked at all the stuff on these shelves, and he seemed to say, "Jennifer, I know why it's so packed in here. Sometimes you're loading up your shelves because you want people to think you're awesome. And sometimes you're loading these shelves to demonstrate your love for *me*. But you must stop. These shelves weren't built to carry that kind of weight. I see all that you're doing, but there's one thing you keep overlooking. You don't overlook your love for people, and you don't overlook your love for me. But you are actually missing the most important thing of all. The most important thing about you isn't how much love you get from people. It's not even about how much you love me. The most important thing is *how much I love you.*"

Identify Your True Identity

Working hard is one way of saying to the people we love, "Look how much I care. I am going to burn the candle at both ends because I love you that much."

We say the same thing to Jesus: "I'm going to say yes to everything, Jesus, because I want you to know how much I love you."

I like that about us—that our hearts drive us toward making the world a lovelier place. But our hard work shouldn't come from the desire to *prove* our love. Instead, when we are at our best, our work ought to be a response to the love we've *already been given* by God.

In other words, our work can't be the source of our identity. Our work should be an *extension* of our truest identity: in Christ.

The question of identity is critically important to address in a book like this. Why? Because the stuff we want to control is defaced with the graffiti of our personal identity crisis. How can we tell if we are people in crisis? Because when we are honest with ourselves, we see areas underneath the graffiti that we are unwilling to surrender to Jesus. We want to handle it ourselves and have spray-painted those corners with the word *Mine*.

To get our control under control, we've got to get honest with ourselves about our identity and our motives. Let's ask ourselves the following questions:

Do I work this hard because it flows from Christ's power within me? Or do I work this hard because I don't know who I really am if I don't keep pushing?

Do I raise my children in partnership with God? Or do I manage outcomes for them—refusing to let them fail, rescuing them at every turn—because I have accidentally made myself into a little savior for those I love?

Who am I, really?

Control Freaks We Can't Help but Love

- Leslie Knope from *Parks and Recreation*: If something needs to be improved, call Leslie. "I took your idea and I made it better," she once said, along with this: "I am big enough to admit that I am often inspired by myself."

- Monica from *Friends*: She has eleven categories for towels.

- Joan Harris from *Mad Men*: "I'm in charge of thinking of things before people know they need them."

- Hermione from *Harry Potter*: "You're saying it wrong. It's Levi-OOOH-sa, not Levio-SA."

- Rabbit from *Winnie the Pooh*: He gets so frustrated when people mess up his garden.

- Sheldon Cooper from *The Big Bang Theory*: Sheldon once made his roommate sign an agreement dictating the time he could use the bathroom.

- Jack Byrnes from *Meet the Parents*: Jack, played by Robert De Niro, made his daughter's boyfriend take a polygraph test.

- Randall Pearson from *This Is Us*: His wife asks, "What are you writing, babe?" He responds, "A list of reasons I'm mad at my mother. I've got twenty-two so far."

Along comes John, the disciple whom Jesus loved, to show us the way.

Flip to the last of the four Gospels, written by this disciple. John was a dear friend of Jesus, one of the closest, and it's indisputable that he loved Jesus deeply. Skim through the pages to see proof of John's love for Jesus. How close he kept himself to the Teacher! See how John loved Jesus so much that he sat next to him at the table in the upper room, how John was the disciple who stayed near the cross as Jesus died. At the end of his life, Jesus asked John to help care for his mother, Mary. The Gospel of John reveals the disciple's great love for the Master.

But—get this—John doesn't describe himself primarily as someone who loves Jesus. Instead, he identifies himself primarily as "the disciple whom Jesus loved." This phrasing appears nowhere else in the Bible except in the Gospel of John. John describes himself this way, not once, but five times.

I confess: John's characterization of himself as "the disciple whom Jesus loved" used to strike me as arrogant. *Who did John think he was anyway? Did he see himself as Jesus' favorite?*

My analysis was all wrong. As it turns out, John simply knew he was God's beloved. So when he picked words to describe himself, John chose words revealing his core identity.

Jesus was the defining relationship in John's life; therefore, John described himself as a person loved by the Savior. We will always surrender our lives to the defining loves and influences in our lives.

What's first place in our lives? Whatever places *first* controls us *most*.

Because John saw Jesus as the first-place force of love in his life, John would have been willing to surrender control to him. In every chapter of his Gospel, John reveals Jesus' deity, showing that he knew who Jesus really is. John understood what it looked like to let go of control and leave matters in God's hands. He realized that his work was an extension of his core identity, not the other way around.

John functioned in life as "the disciple whom Jesus loved."

I feel bad picking on Peter, but I'm guessing that Peter might have described himself as "the disciple who loves Jesus" instead of "the disciple whom Jesus loved."

Peter took dramatic actions to demonstrate that love. He exhibited a tendency to impulsively control situations as proof of his love for Jesus. Peter pulled out a sword to show his love. He jumped out of the boat to prove it.

"I will lay down my life for you" (John 13:37).

"We have left everything to follow you!" (Matthew 19:27).

"Even if all fall away, I will not" (Mark 14:29).

Imagine—Peter was trying to control the outcomes for Jesus! Before we judge him too harshly, let's remember that he, like John, loved his Master. No doubt he fully intended to forsake everything for Jesus. But like Peter, don't we sometimes cross the line out of love for another? We can do real damage when we try to be someone else's savior.

Consider the mental shift that happens when we focus primarily on Jesus' love for us instead of our love for Jesus.

Rather than working to prove our love, we work because Jesus has *already* proven his love toward us.

Here's what this might look like in an everyday situation. Someone asks if you'd be willing to sign up to bring two dozen cookies as treats for the kindergarten graduation. You absolutely don't have time because you work a full-time job and you already agreed to work at the elementary book fair. You want to say no, but you feel like you'll let people down if you don't say yes. You're worried that if you say no, you'll look like a bad mom. So you agree to bring the cookies.

In the end, your yes becomes about proving yourself and proving your love.

We do so much proving.

Proving to the boss. Proving to our parents. Proving to the employees. Proving to the stockholders. Proving to the other moms at the classroom party. Proving to Jesus.

Peter was a prover. He totally would have signed up to bring the cookies.

John might have been more likely to pause and respond to requests for his time by filtering them through his core identity: "I am the disciple whom Jesus loved." If our relationship to Jesus is our defining one, then every decision—big or little—passes through that filter. So instead of saying yes to prove our love and devotion to people or to Jesus, we are allowed to experience the freedom of saying no, based on the fact that we have nothing to prove. We already *are* beloved.

Our actions in life will always follow our choices. Our first decision is choosing our primary identity. Our calendar is not our primary identity. Our caregiving is not our primary identity. Our productivity is not our primary identity. Being "awesome" is not our primary identity. As daughters of God, our primary identity is Jesus. His power, then, extends over us, our work, our priorities, our everything.

Here's a great way to figure out what your primary identity truly is. Ask yourself: "What are the things that, if they were taken away, would shatter the identity I have created?"

Is it your work? Your calendar? Your efforts to shield your children from pain? This urge to always say yes?

For my part, I didn't realize how much my identity was tied to my work until I left the newsroom for the farm. And then it took me years to see how I'd built a new identity around my ministry work. One form of work perhaps looked holier than the other, but in both cases, I found myself experiencing a case of mistaken identity—estimating my worth based on my usefulness.

And that's where I found myself on the beginning of this journey—tired, exhausted, and trying to find a way to lay down everything that threatened my truest identity.

Control has always been a matter of the heart. For me, the battle for my heart is regularly fought inside the tiny squares of my to-do list. The momentum for this battle shifts in God's favor when I settle the issue of identity.

Let this be our battle cry: "I am the disciple whom Jesus loves."

It's Okay to Course-Correct

I'm on this journey with you, daily reclaiming my right identity. Whatever places *first* controls me *most*. I frequently have to course-correct when I veer to old patterns. But even when I backslide, I find myself irrevocably loved. Yes, even then.

While reading about "the disciple whom Jesus loved," I found a beautiful surprise in the original Greek. Literally rendered, the verses can be translated "the disciple whom Jesus *kept on loving.*"[3]

Jesus. Keeps. On. Loving. Us. His love for us isn't conditional.

When we take on too much, he keeps on loving us.

When we get in over our heads, he keeps on loving us.

When we need a course correction, he keeps on loving us.

When we overcommit, he keeps on loving us.

When we underdeliver, he keeps on loving us.

When we say yes, he keeps on loving us.

When we say no, he keeps on loving us.

When we ridiculously believe the control is all ours, he keeps on loving us.

And when we finally realize it's not, he keeps on loving us.

What a relief.

Friend, I see you. You need that kind of relief.

You need to know that no matter what, Jesus keeps on loving you.

I see you in the grocery aisle, in the line at the bank, at the end of the bleachers, and out on Facebook. Behind that thin smile, I see the weariness you carry. You're trying to do all the right things, to keep the kids happy, the lawn mowed, the schedule organized. Things are crazy at work . . . and when was the last time someone offered you a simple thank-you?

I see you. I see how you pay the high cost of being awesome. I see how you do all that you do because you love your people, and you love your Jesus.

You're not even sure you're that great of a Jesus girl, seeing how you missed your quiet time for the fourth day in a row. Your prayer life feels stale. And who can find quiet in the chaos of your days? Who can find a spare five minutes to be still?

But I see something more in you that maybe you don't see right now. I wish you could see it too. I see a warrior spirit inside you. You are strong for so many people. In your home, you are nurse, cook, launderer, entertainer, psychologist, taxi driver. In your friendships, you are comedian, helper, shoulder to cry on. You are wise. You are funny. You don't take the beatings that this world dishes out, and you're the first to defend the underdog. That's no small thing.

Go easy on yourself, dear heart. You are the disciple whom Jesus loves.

Do you know that?

And you are the disciple *whom Jesus keeps on loving.*

Because of his unceasing love for you, sometimes he's going to ask you to say no. He will empower you to do it. Other times, he will ask you to give your brave yes. But don't let your worth be tied to how well you come through for people. Don't let your motivation be "I have to do this, or no one else will."

Let all that you do be a response to Jesus' love for you. Every day, you and I can begin to see ourselves as the recipients of God's love rather than as machines who need to push and hustle and control in order to find the love and meaning we're all after.

We are not pixels. We are people.

Our robust inner control freaks will feel the external pressure to say yes because we don't want to disappoint anyone and we don't want to be called lazy. But look, your essential self will step out from behind all of that productivity to say, "Here I am, the disciple whom Jesus keeps on loving, no matter what." Even if you disappoint someone. Even if someone calls you lazy.

Friend, you are doing better than you think you are. It's all under control. Invite Jesus into your pantry, let him rearrange what's on the shelves, and then let him whisper these words over you: "You are the disciple whom I love, and I will keep on loving you."

Cracking the Control Code ∧∧∧∧∧∧∧∧∧∧∧∧

1. **Who are you?** Cracking the control code will require each of us to take a sober assessment of our identity. What makes you who you are?

   If you feel stumped as you consider that question, think of it another way by asking yourself this: "What are the things that, if they were taken away, would shatter the identity I have created?"

   To spark your thinking, consider your work, your family, your relationships, the stuff you own, the way you look, the longings you have.

   One by one, commit to turning over control in each of those areas to God.

   Begin to make your primary identity this: "The one whom Jesus keeps on loving."

2. **Identity experiment.** Anywhere your identity is challenged, post a note with the words, "My identity is found in Jesus" or "Jesus keeps on loving me." If your identity is tied to your work, put the note on your cubicle wall. If your identity is tied to your looks, put it on your mirror. If it's tied to your parenting, put it on the dashboard of your minivan. Read the statement again and again until that truth sinks into your marrow. You can find printable notes on my website at www.ItsAllUnderControlBook.com/Resources.

4

Superpowers

Uncovering Your Strengths, Your Kryptonite, and That Line We All Tend to Cross

∧∧∧∧

RECENTLY A BLOGGER interviewed me via e-mail. She asked a great question: "What counsel would you give to the woman who wants to leave behind the life of hustling, efficiency, and busyness for a life of rest and grace?"

So much weariness sits behind her question. In fact, you may have picked up this book because you're looking for the answer to it. It's exhausting to feel like you're on the hook for everything.

When she asked me how to leave behind that kind of life, I let the question roll around in my mind for several days. During that time, my life was a mix of hustle, busyness, and efficiency while I:

- Helped plan a surprise birthday party for a friend
- Finished a chapter for this book
- Raced a sick kitten to the vet for IVs and wept with my daughters for five hours straight while the kitten slowly died despite lifesaving efforts
- Made eye appointments for the girls
- Visited the orthodontist
- Helped our younger daughter figure out how to use her new albuterol inhaler
- Drove our older daughter to a spiritual retreat
- Launched a fund-raiser on my blog for a nonprofit
- Selected worship songs for our church
- Weeded landscaping beds
- Took care of an extra child for a day while her mother went through medical testing
- Made plans for an upcoming trip to the lake
- Sent a series of encouraging text messages to a young woman I mentor

I'm guessing your list looks similar to mine. The details are different, but we're both operating on the same level of crazy. Life ain't a walk in the park, is it, amigos? During those three days, the blogger's question would rise up. I asked myself: *So, Jennifer, how do you leave behind a life of busyness to find rest? Your own life has been a series of one activity after another!* I sat down at my computer after three days, tucked strands of hair behind my ears, and typed the answer that had become clear to me:

You don't have to leave it *all* behind for rest. In fact, that's going to be unrealistic. Yes, God's definitely going to ask you to lay down some stuff, but he also created you to be an efficient, productive woman capable of doing great things.

God hasn't given us the task of fixing everything, but make no mistake, he's not calling us to lie limply on the floor either. He's calling us to do the incredible work of making better what he's put within our reach. He's calling us to rise up.

It's hard to know when to hold tight to what we love and when to let it go. So I pray, "Give us the wisdom today, dear Jesus, to know the difference."[1]

Even though my life was busy, I couldn't fathom crossing off any of those thirteen items. That list was part of God's race set out for me. When I said yes to everything on that list, I was saying yes to God.

I am self-aware enough to know that I am an achiever and that I need more chill in my life, but I'm not sure I will always get a free pass on busyness. (Trust me, we'll devote whole chapters to rest, waiting on God, figuring out how to say no better, and setting good boundaries. Those will come later.)

Furthermore, I take great joy in moments when I'm charged up and living my calling. Did you know that it's actually okay to feel that way? Did you know that you can be an achiever and love Jesus at the same time? Sometimes I get the feeling that Christian women think we must down-play our ambition. We act like we can earn spiritual brownie points if we diminish our gifts, because we've been taught not to trust our motives regarding our accomplishments. As a result, the concept of rest gets elevated as the pinnacle of a life in Jesus, and anything that looks like achievement becomes synonymous with conceit.

But that's not fair to God's creative genius at work within us. You are not called to shrink. You are called to shine. Sure, you've gotta rest, girl. But you are also called to the meaning-ful work of leading and teaching and healing and helping and fighting for what's right.

God equipped you to do the incredible work of making better what he's put within your reach. Let's figure out how to do *that*.

God Wants You to Be a Partner, Not a Player

You may remember the parable of the loaned money, which Jesus shares with his followers in Matthew 25. In the story, Jesus introduces us to four characters: the master and his three servants. The master has a lot of money, and because he's about to go on a long trip, he asks his servants to take care of it while he's away. The first two servants partner with the master by investing the money that the master has placed in their care. The third servant buries his money. When the master returns, the servants tell the master what they did.

The first two eagerly share how their investments produced nice returns. The master is pleased, telling both of them, "Good work! You did your job well. From now on be my partner" (Matthew 25:21, MSG).

Be my partner. My heart's desire is to hear those same words from God. I want to partner with God in whatever *he* cares about most. That partnership will require me to make an investment—just like the servants were asked to do. I invest what God has given me—my time, my calendar, my gifts, my energy, and yes, even my ambition—so I can join him in the work he asks me to do. Sometimes that work is grueling. Sometimes that work has me in tears. Sometimes I'm dropping into bed at 11:30 p.m., weary but feeling contentment in knowing I partnered with God.

I don't want to be like the third servant, the one who buried the money. I'll be honest with you, though. For years, I empathized with this servant. The master was furious with him, and when I would read the master's angry response, I would think, *Wow, God. That's pretty harsh. Wasn't he just trying to protect what the master had given him? What's wrong with playing it safe?*

I was wrong. The gospel doesn't ask us to play it safe. Lately I've seen evidence that people actually *do* believe in a gospel of safe living and personal comfort—and maybe I've been one of those people. Have you seen it? It's a type of Western-world Christianity that promotes "self-care" more than taking up the cross—as if "resting in Jesus" means we need to take more naps and book weekly massages. (I love both, by the way.) But God doesn't call us to risk-free living.

Here's what the master says about playing it safe: "That's a terrible way to live! It's criminal to live cautiously like that! If you knew I was after the best, why did you do less than the least?" (Matthew 25:26, MSG).

The third servant was merely a player when it came to working on his master's behalf. He took what his master had entrusted to him and hid it underground because he thought he knew what was best. In essence, he was playing God instead of partnering with him. He gave "less than the least." He gained nothing *because he risked nothing*.

What does this lesson mean for us? We are called to risk something. As partners with God, we are called to invest what the Master has given to us. That's the surprising truth about surrender that we rarely hear—or at least that I rarely heard.

I hope there's some freedom for you in this, particularly if you've been shamed by pious-sounding people who give you the side-eye for being "overly ambitious." Hear me now: There is so much good about you. The Master has given you much to invest! He is inviting you: "Be my partner."

God actually built women like you for this terrific alliance. Women like you are the ones I want looking over my taxes before the paperwork is sent to the IRS. You are the ones I want reviewing my mammogram. I want friends in my life who won't give up on me easily. Trust me: You are the kind of women I want editing this book before it lands on a bookshelf.

I am not a proponent of doing it all, all of the time. But

I am a proponent of doing it well when we're called into service.

The trouble with women like us is this: We're doing a lot of things, but often we're doing them without joy. God didn't intend it that way. When we enter into a true partnership with him, as servants who invest what he's given us, there's a real reward for us. In this same parable, the master says to the two partnering servants: "Let's celebrate together!" (Matthew 25:23, NLT). Other Bible translations put it this way: "Enter into the joy of your master" (ESV) and "Come and share your master's happiness!" (NIV).

In short, when we stop playing God and start partnering with him, the story gets really good.

But you and I both know we have a tendency to go overboard. How do we make sure we don't go too far, so we can hang on to our joy as we partner with him? We watch for these warning signs:

- ▶ We are functioning within our call, but we don't feel fulfilled.
- ▶ We feel like we can't trust other people to do their jobs, so we take over, denying people the opportunity to live into their own callings.
- ▶ We subscribe to the notion that "I'm capable, therefore I should," so we say yes to it all.
- ▶ We become accidental supervisors of everything and everyone.

- ▸ Because we want to give our all, we often feel powerless to say no. We say yes to every assignment, not pausing long enough to see if God intends us to commit to one more thing.
- ▸ We are scared that if we decline, we'll appear either cowardly or inadequate. So we add another heaping spoonful to an already-overloaded plate, which we try to carry one-handed across a tightrope, all the while telling the world, "It's fine. I've got it all under control."

We've got to get our control under control, so it doesn't take control of us. We must not confuse our God-given abilities with our God-given assignments.

As I told the blogger who interviewed me, it can be hard to know when to charge forward and when to step back. So I continue to pray this prayer every day: "Give me the wisdom today, dear Jesus, to know the difference."

Let's listen for his answer. He still speaks to us, twenty-first century women.

A New Way to Understand Control

What if God actually knew what he was doing when he made you? What if God made you the way you are for a reason? What if he actually created you as a responsible, forward-thinking, and dependable human so that you could carry out your one-of-a-kind calling in this world? What if you aren't a person to be "fixed," but a person whose gifts and desires simply need to be rechanneled?

Caveat: Unchecked, the things that make you *you* could actually harm you and the people you love when you enter into a state of overcontrol. But channeled correctly, the way God made you . . . *is actually your superpower.*

You want to partner with God. You don't intend to play God. You probably have a deep longing to actively do what God called you to—but you've seen how your do-ing sometimes causes harm. You want your do-ing to neither harm those you love nor break your communion with God. You want your do-ing to give your life meaning rather than run you ragged. Yet you sometimes cross the line.

Me too, friend. I wondered: *How can I identify that line that I find myself repeatedly crossing?*

I wasn't satisfied with the notion that anyone who had the occasional control-freak episode was a narcissistic jerk. I began to think about some of the most gifted and talented women I know. They are women who have an astonishing ability to strategize, organize, and mobilize.

Yet when they are under stress or operating from misguided thinking, they swing toward unhealthy control. I saw the same tendency in myself. When I am in a healthy state of control, partnering with God, my days are filled with meaning and purpose—even amidst the busy. Then the line gets crossed. In that moment, I'm in urgent need of a paper bag for breathing and someone sane to collect my children for the night.

As I thought about the times I overreacted, I realized that it was usually the little things that set me off. I could juggle five demanding tasks at once and actually handle crisis remarkably well, all things considered. But if I lost my car keys or sunglasses, I'd enter DEFCON 3. In moments of stress, I would stop partnering with God and start playing God.

I wondered, *How can I be a partner instead of a player? How can I work with God and the way he made me rather than work against him and his purposes?*

Getting there demanded a new way of understanding the triggers that cause you and me to try controlling what we shouldn't. First, I considered the reasons people seek control and realized they vary. Remember the consummate planner on your college dorm floor whom everyone flocked to for printer paper or quarters for the washing machine? Then there was the coworker at your first job who brought in a cake for everyone's birthday (including her own, so no one else would have to). And you're still in awe of the aunt who always looked as if she just stepped off a fashion runway.

Nothing ever seemed outside of their control—yet their focus and motivations were different. Maybe you also noticed that their greatest assets could morph into liabilities when taken to an extreme. Your dorm mate not only provided change; she also began removing and folding your clothes if you didn't promptly remove them from the dryer—then charged you a fee for her "service." Maybe your kind coworker tried a little too hard to set you up on dates with her bachelor nephew. And your aunt might have turned a new shade of crimson when she showed up to a family wedding and discovered someone else wearing the same dress. Hit any of these folks' triggers, and things might not look pretty.

Once I'd thought about the different strengths and weaknesses of people who seek control, I identified three categories of people who want to keep it all under control. I call them Drivers, Devoters, and Darlings. Each group values something slightly different. When they are operating from their superpower, we can't help but marvel at their accomplishments. Yet when taken to an extreme, that strength can become their kryptonite, causing them to break down, shut down, or come down hard on the people they care about:

The Drivers. Drivers value meeting goals, being efficient, and maintaining external order. They are decisive, confident, methodical long-range planners who are zealously committed to whatever God calls them into.

Despite their many strengths, Drivers are triggered by people who don't pull their weight, or by emergencies or roadblocks they didn't see coming. Their tendency to say yes to every request can make them their own worst enemies, preventing them from delegating or relaxing and causing their anxiety to spike whenever things don't go according to plan—or when they even ruminate on what might go wrong.

The Devoters. Devoters' priority is guarding the welfare of those they love most. As a result, they are caring, generous, and loyal. They pick up on others' needs and freely give to those around them.

The Devoters' self-sacrifice can turn into self-sabotage when they wear themselves out or become overbearing. They are sometimes set off by friends and family who refuse their help, and they may stunt the development of family members by going overboard in trying to make life easy for them.

The Darlings. Darlings seek to be the best version of themselves; as a result, they are more focused on controlling themselves than others. They hold fast to strict standards of personal integrity and behavior, making them dependable, hardworking, well-liked members of any team.

Watch out, however, when they discover that they are unable to meet all the unrealistic expectations they've set for themselves, which may lead to feelings of worthlessness. At this point, their perfectionistic, people-pleasing tendencies may go into overdrive, leaving them frustrated and burned out.

Do you see some of the Driver, Devoter, or Darling in yourself? As you think about the three types, keep a few points in mind:

- None of the three types is better or worse than the others.
- You are a complicated, beautiful, multilayered person.

- ► Not every characteristic in any of the profiles will
  resonate with you.
- ► You might see parts of yourself in the descriptions
  of more than one type, and your type can change in
  different seasons of life.

Knowing my triggers has helped me take better control over my need for control. I think it might do the same for you, so I've included longer descriptions of each type on pages 257–264. For fun, you might visit www.ItsAllUnder ControlBook.com/Resources to take the Control Character Quiz, which I created to help you figure out which type best describes you.

As you continue to move through this book, keep these profiles in mind. Whether you're primarily a Driver, a Devoter, or a Darling, you have so much to contribute to this world, for God's glory. Once you begin to see the external and internal triggers that cause you to grab for control when it isn't yours, you'll be better able to relinquish it.

Welcome to self-discovery. Welcome to becoming a better human. Isn't this fun?

Cracking the Control Code ∧∧∧∧∧∧∧∧∧∧∧∧∧∧∧

Discover your control character. Before you read any further, take a few minutes to read the more complete descriptions of each of the three types of characters beginning on page 257. Do you see yourself in any of these types? Perhaps you see a bit of yourself in all three. For fun, visit www.ItsAllUnderControlBook.com/Resources to take the Control Character Quiz. Do not be alarmed if your control character shifts over time, or if you see yourself in more than one character type. No longer will you be in the dark about why you do what you do or how you see the world. Armed with this information, you can partner with God instead of playing God.

5

Hang On

Finding the Courage to Do Really Hard Things

∧∧∧∧

SOMETIMES "LET GO AND LET GOD" is bad advice.

Let's all take a deep breath and not let that sentence scare us.

You probably picked up this book because you're tired of feeling like you're on the hook for everything. Yet "let go and let God" sounds impractical. What does that even mean?

I asked myself the same question after I said yes to that irresistible invitation from Jesus. After accepting his offer, I knew I needed to open my hands to him. God can't put anything into these hands when they are tightened into fists.

I want to trust God with all that I have and all that I am. I don't want to keep my fists closed around my preferences. There's definitely stuff I need to let go of. My inner Driver needs to let go of worry, outcomes, an overscheduled life, my ideas of success. My inner Devoter needs to let go of the belief that I'm single-handedly in charge of my kids' spiritual growth. And my inner Darling needs to let go of the desire to win your approval.

Yet I can't shake this truth: It's anti-gospel to simply "let go" of it all. Picking up crosses and following Jesus is the hardest work we will ever know. We can't divorce ourselves from responsibility, nor would we want to. We are the women who aren't afraid of a challenge, who aren't afraid of hard work, and who make an impact on this world when we operate with our God-given superpowers as Drivers, Devoters, and Darlings.

Furthermore, some of what we're called to do on a daily basis is actually quite satisfying, and I don't feel like God wants me to "let go" of that. (I don't apologize for the fact that I am as excited at eight o'clock on a Monday morning as some people are at five o'clock on a Friday afternoon.)

The question, then, is this: When do we let go, and when do we hang on?

Most Christians I know are very uncomfortable with the idea that God might actually want us to hang on to anything at all. It feels like an affront to his sovereignty. I know this because I have been one of those people. I own a mug that says, "Let Go and Let God." I have titled several blog posts using those five words. I've probably whispered that phrase to a dozen friends over the years. They needed more than a cliché, but it's all I had at the time. And as a result, I probably have some apologizing to do.

I understand why "letting go" becomes our default phrase when we want to live surrendered to Jesus. "Letting go" definitely sounds more Jesus-approved than "hanging on." Hanging on feels tight and squeezed. It feels like someone stuffed eight bags of kitty litter in a duffel bag and asked us to carry it across Manhattan. It feels like we're trying to run the show or like we think God clocked out for the weekend. It's all on you and me, baby.

But the phrase "let go and let God" continues to befuddle so many women I know (though we might be afraid to confess it during Tuesday night Bible study). We don't know how to practically *do* what those words ask of us. We can't walk away from every difficult relationship, for instance. We can't ignore the phone, the list of obligations, our God-given calling to help take care of our square of the earth and dependent humans in diapers.

Imagine you are standing at a crossroads with signs pointing in two directions. One is marked "Let go." The other is marked "Hang on." You think you have to pick one direction and walk that way forever. That's not true.

Here's the truth that no one ever tells us—or at least that no one ever told me: You don't have to pick one road and walk that path for the rest of your life. Gospel living is not an either/or question. It's both/and. It's coming back to that fork in the road every day—with every decision, every obligation, and every relationship—and asking God to help you choose.

This is the crossroads where we finally learn what's ours to control, and what's not. To be truly surrendered to Christ, sometimes you've got to walk the road that says "Hang on." When you walk that road, you will have to hang on tighter than you thought you could. Other times, you'll have to walk the road of letting go.

How will you know which way to walk? You'll know because you don't stand at the crossroads alone, left to your own devices. "Your teacher will be right there, local and on the job, urging you on whenever you wander left or right: 'This is the right road. Walk down this road'" (Isaiah 30:21, MSG).

In a moment of clarity, you will know which way to go. That direction may come after reading Scripture or praying, talking with a trusted friend or mentor, or experiencing a change in circumstances. (In chapter 6, I'll also introduce you to the Decision Tree, a tool I use to filter requests for my time or attention.) When that clarity comes, trust the wisdom that God has given you, as scary as it is, and then take the next step. As you step out in faith, God's peace will prevail—and that peace can come both in the letting go and in the hanging on. Sometimes the Spirit will guide you to let go, even though you've always thought the only godly response was to hang on. You've got to know that there are times in your life when what you're hanging on to is unhealthy. We'll talk about letting go in the next chapter.

But sometimes, the Spirit will say to you, *Don't you dare let go. I will help you hang on tight.* As the great prophet Kenny

Rogers once said, "You got to know when to hold 'em, know when to fold 'em."

The Hard Work of Hanging On

The day was cool and foggy, like all the clouds had fallen to kiss the streets of San Francisco. I had come to this iconic city with girlfriends, and we took it all in: the wharf, the bridges, the blue Pacific stretching out to forever. We lingered at sidewalk cafés and little flower stands. A lifelong Iowan, I felt like I had landed on a new planet: a shimmering city set on a thousand hills, all enveloped by mist. We took several trips on cable cars, riding up and down hilly tracks. The view from the cable car was, of course, spectacular. If there was room for me on the cable car platform, I loved standing on it, right on the edge, holding tightly to the shiny handles, skimming over the streets while the wind whistled in my ears. As we crested each hill, San Francisco opened her arms wider, revealing more and more of the breathtaking bay and Alcatraz Island, which rose up like a fortress from the water.

During one cable car trip, there was no room for me on the platform, so I sat near the driver, watching with interest as he operated it. Cable car drivers are called gripmen because, as the name suggests, they are in charge of a lever that controls the "grip," a viselike mechanism that latches on to the cable like a giant pair of pliers. The job of latching on to the cable requires terrific upper body strength from the gripmen, who hold the lever. If their hold on the lever is too weak, the grip mechanism will not be able to grab the cable tightly, and it will slip on the cable. When that happens, the gripmen have to stop, back the car down the hill, and start over.

There comes a point when the gripmen will eventually let go of the lever in their hands, but for long stretches of the journey, they have to do this: hang on tight.

That's the way it is for us.

There will be times when you simply can't let go. You've got to hang on tight, as if your life depends upon it. It will feel like you've hitched a ride on the back side of a hurricane. Your hands will get calloused and cramped. This isn't the kind of surrender we usually hear about, is it? This kind of sweat-on-the-brow surrender is fiery and wild. It will ask so much of you that it will hurt.

Perhaps you will be able to let go later. But not yet.

Don't let go when it gets difficult. Let go only when it's time.

Until then, hang on.

I understand how tempting it is to quit, especially when it's hard.

Let's have a frank conversation here about "letting go." Letting go can easily become a defeatist response to avoid the pain of holding on. It can be a knee-jerk reaction when we are certain that we don't have it in us to hang on anymore. Honestly, when we talk ourselves into "letting go," sometimes it's a way of spiritualizing an exit from the hard stuff.

Think back to times when you've heard (or said) comments like these:

"I thought God wanted me to pursue grad school,
 but it's so hard, and I can't keep up with the work.
 Maybe I should quit and trust that God has another
 door open for me." So we let go.

"This election is a disaster, so I'm not voting. I'm going
 to 'let go and let God' because he's got it all under
 control." Again, we let go.

"I'm so mad at my church friends. Starting next Sunday,
 I'm done with this church." Once more, we let go.

"What's happening in [insert name of developing
 country] is really sad. I'm glad God has this situation
 under control." You can see where this is headed.
 Feeling absolved by God's sovereignty, people might
 brush their hands together, avert their eyes, and walk
 away without taking needed action.

Do we let go because it's too hard to hang on? Do we
let go because it's too messy? "Letting go" can be the escape
hatch we take so that we feel justified in backing away.

"I'm done," we say. "God's got this."

It's absolutely true that our sovereign God is in control of
our relationships, kids, and finances. It's also true that God
can single-handedly do anything he chooses to resolve social
injustice and world hunger. But before you let go, ask yourself if God is calling you into the hard work of hanging on.
In this age, he tends to use Spirit-empowered people to do
his work—*the hard work of hanging on*—to make a broken
world better.

God can perform any miracle he wants, but what if that miracle is you? What if God is calling you to be an everyday gripman, to partner with him to keep the car on the track?

God works in so many ways, and quite often, he does that work through *actual human beings* who are willing to show up when it's inconvenient. We can't afford to hide behind God's sovereignty when he's calling us onto the battlefield.

That truth is vividly illustrated in a parable-like story I heard years ago about a Christian man caught in a storm with extreme flooding. Despite warnings to leave his home, the man decided to wait the storm out and trust God to save him through divine intervention.

Neighbors offered to drive the man away from oncoming floodwaters. But he declined, saying he had faith God would save him.

Next, someone in a canoe paddled by his house, offering him a ride as the waters continued to rise. The man declined, saying he had faith God would save him.

The waters rose higher, so he climbed onto his roof. A helicopter pilot dropped a rope ladder, but still the man refused, saying he had faith God would save him.

The man drowned.

In heaven, the man asked God, "I put my faith in you, so why didn't you save me?"

God responded, "I sent you a car. I sent you a canoe. I sent you a helicopter. What else were you looking for?"

God sends help through ordinary people called into service. Sometimes you will be the miracle for other people.

Sometimes other people will be the miracle for you. They will show up with a car, a ladder, a foil-covered casserole dish, a hug. And in that moment, you'll be so grateful that someone cared enough to commit to the hard work of hanging on. For you.

When the Middle Is the Hardest

I know how hard it is. Hanging on is painful, especially when you're in the middle.

For instance, in work projects, I'm a great starter. And if I get to the end, I'm a decent finisher. But I can be downright awful in the middle—when the sparkle of the beginning has long since faded and the finish line is a speck in the distance.

Take marriage, for instance.

I remember the picture-perfect start after my wedding to Scott:

Our reception was held in an old gymnasium in Marathon, Iowa, a block from the home where I grew up. It was the gym where I played seventh-grade basketball, where I attended my first prom. With a small army of volunteers, we transformed the gym into a wedding hall. Miles of crepe paper were draped around that stinky gym in an act of decorating prowess that would have sent Pinterest into a tailspin of horror. Our dinner reception was served by a bunch of middle-aged fellows wearing greasy aprons who worked with Dad at the farmers' grain cooperative. They grilled turkey fillets. Potato salad was heaped in cumulonimbus clumps upon flimsy plastic plates.

To us, it felt first-class fancy—this unglamorous wedding reception, lit up with thousands of twinkling lights strung from the basketball hoops to the fake ficus trees. It was a fairy-tale beginning to what—we hoped—would be our happily ever after.

We danced until midnight under the rafters. When the band slowed things down a bit, I nestled my head under Scott's chin, feeling his warm breath coming out in long exhales into my hair, as the vocalist crooned into the microphone, "Could I have this dance for the rest of my life?"

That was the beginning. Hanging on looked romantic, effortless.

Then came the middle.

The needle scratched across the record. It didn't happen in a day, but in a series of months that turned to years. We woke up and realized that someone had short-circuited the electricity in the marriage, and we both blamed the other person for faulty wiring.

The middle was hard. There were nights where we yelled the dreaded *d*-word—*divorce*—even though neither of us truly meant it. Whole seasons passed where it seemed as if we couldn't agree on anything: next stops in the career, the color of the drapes, politics. In the midst of heated arguments, it felt like letting go would have been the easier choice—particularly the week we decided to work together to tile and grout the bathroom floor. (Pro tip: If you care about your marriage, don't take on a tiling project together.)

Yes, hanging on is hard in the middle. At the altar, we

pledged "for better or for worse." In the midst of the struggle, we discovered that sometimes, the better comes *after* the worse.

Technically, Scott and I are still in the "middle." We are more than two decades past our grand start, and, God willing, we are still decades from the finish.

This is what's keeping our marriage strong in the middle: the hard work of hanging on. This is not prescriptive for those of you who are in abusive relationships. By all means, *no*. What I am saying is this: Just because something is hard work doesn't mean it's wrong or should be abandoned.

Maybe one of these situations sounds familiar to you:

You start a new job with great anticipation, but you are suddenly overwhelmed by the responsibility. *It's hard work.*

You begin writing a book, starting an overseas mission, getting your degree, but when you think you're close to a breakthrough, you see a giant hill up ahead. *It's hard work.*

At the starting line of a marriage, your "I do" carries all of your best hopes. But

What to Hang On To

- ▶ The belief that change is possible
- ▶ The people who see the best in you
- ▶ The people who hold you accountable
- ▶ What God has put within your reach to care for
- ▶ The hope that hard work today can make a better tomorrow
- ▶ Work that you love
- ▶ Work that is hard
- ▶ The hope of the Cross
- ▶ The hand of your God

months or years later, marriage isn't all that you thought it would be. *It's hard work.*

When hard times come, the temptation to quit will be great. In those moments, most of us will ask God to take the hardest parts away. But deep inside of us, we want more than an easier life: We want Jesus to prove himself bigger than the struggle.

When you want to quit, hear God speak with blazing urgency: "Do not give up" (2 Chronicles 15:7).

I love how those verses are translated in the English Standard Version: "But you, take courage! Do not let your hands be weak, for your work shall be rewarded."

Refuse to give in to the temptation to give up. Refuse to pray only for the hard to go away. Pray for a faith bigger than the hard. "Do not let your hands be weak." Pray for hands that will grip tight when God tells you to hang on.

Hang on. Yes, it's hard, but it might not be time to let go.

Hang on. You might be the miracle someone was praying for.

Hang on. This might be only a season, with relief around the corner.

Hang on. A great crowd of witnesses is cheering for you.

Hang on. When you hang on with bravery, you emotionally strengthen others who are struggling to hang on themselves. You're showing them that it's possible to do hard things.

Hang on. If you are uniquely positioned to do something to make the world a better place, even if it's hard, you should do it.

Hang on. For your marriage. For your kids. For your church. For the people that your ministry bravely serves. For the hurting. For your friends who don't know if they can hang on anymore.

Hang on. Because Jesus will meet you in the middle of your hardest battles.

Some struggles aren't resolved in a day. Many heartfelt prayers aren't quickly answered. In that moment you want to quit, wait one moment longer because that's often when the miracle happens.

Hang on.

Don't Give Up

Scott and I had to hang on tight a few years ago when uncertainty hit our farm like a punch to the gut. Four days after my accident on that icy highway, Scott's father, Paul, died of leukemia. This meant that Scott would not only grieve the loss of his father and business partner, he would also care for the land alone. A law-school graduate who had only recently decided to return to the farm, Scott was still fairly new to the business. Sure, he'd grown up on this fourth-generation Lee family farm. But it's one thing to haul grain and feed pigs when you're a teenager. It's quite another to make decisions about what kind of seed to use, when to sell your grain, and what to do when your pigs—your own investment—start getting sick.

Paul died in the cold of winter. That spring, we were so grateful for the mercy of God during this trying time. Our crops grew tall, thickening over the rows so everything green was touching. There was something so beautiful and hopeful about that. It felt like everything was going to be okay, even though Paul's old John Deere cap drooped, sad, on a nail by the back door.

We had hope.

But then October came. Not a single plant had been harvested when we awoke one morning to find a thick white blanket of snow covering all the crops. The snow stole the hopefulness we'd felt earlier that year.

Late that afternoon, a farmer who lived a few miles away tapped his knuckles on the back door. I opened it and found him standing on the doormat with his fists shoved into a thick quilted jacket with a corduroy collar. He showed up at our house on a really hard day, during a really hard year.

The farmer's eyes looked softer than I'd remembered.

"Scott home yet?" he asked.

"No," I told him. "Still doing chores."

"Well," the farmer continued, "you just tell him that I stopped by because I want him to know something for certain. I want him to know that the harvest always comes. You'll let him know?"

I nodded my head, feeling a catch in my throat.

The farmer had come to remind us, in his own way, what the Bible says about hope in hard times. "At the proper time we will reap a harvest *if we do not give up*" (Galatians 6:9, emphasis added).

Friend, I don't know what harvest you're waiting for. I

don't know what storm has stolen your hope. Maybe you're reading these words when you're on your last dime, at the end of your frayed rope, or on the ragged brink of your sanity as a stay-at-home mom. God sees you. He sees how you've been pouring into the people you love and what you've been pouring into your everyday work. And he wants you to know that your dedication is not in vain. "At the proper time we will reap a harvest *if we do not give up*."

Don't give up.

Today I'm the friend at your back door, tapping my knuckles to see if you're home. I'm standing here on your doormat to tell you the same thing the old farmer told me: "The harvest always comes."

And I'm here to tell you that the farmer was right. Weeks after he stood on our stoop, the harvest *did* come. The snow melted, and Scott drove the old green combine back and forth across a gently sloping hill the color of a lion's mane and sheared it all.

Don't give up, friend. Hang on when God tells you to hang on. He is still in this.

Today's the day to believe it: At the proper time, you will reap a harvest, just as he promised.

Cracking the Control Code

At the crossroads. When something is really hard, it can be difficult to know whether God wants you to stop or push harder.

Often God will offer a moment of clarity. Sometimes it will come through the wise counsel of a friend, a Scripture verse, or a message from a trusted preacher. Sometimes you will need to take a break in order to gain proper perspective.

Do you have something you're wondering if you need to hang on to? On a slip of paper, write down a word or phrase to represent the situation you're in or the decision you need to make. Stick it in the pages of your Bible like a bookmark near Isaiah 30:21, which reads: "Whether you turn to the right or to the left, your ears will hear a voice behind you, saying, 'This is the way; walk in it.'" Or you can find a beautiful printable of this verse on my website, www.ItsAllUnderControlBook.com/Resources. Print off the verse and post it in a place where you can read it every day.

Each morning for one week, read that verse. Ask God's guidance about the situation on your paper.

If, after a week, you're still having difficulty discerning whether you should hang on or let go, ask yourself these questions:

- *If I let go, will I regret it?*
- *Is the end goal (and the required work) in alignment with my values and biblical principles?*
- *Do I want to stop because it's hard or because it's time?*
- *How do I envision this situation in ten hours? In ten days? In ten years?*

· *Can I envision God, who began a good work in me, carrying this out to completion?*

You may need to consult with people who will be honest with you about whether it's time to quit or keep going. Just because something's hard doesn't mean it's wrong or a mistake. It can be easy to quit when you're discouraged, especially when you don't see desired results.

However, if you are hanging on to something that isn't good for you—such as a toxic or damaging relationship—you may be too close to the situation to see clearly. Ask a counselor or trusted adviser to help you see what you can't see on your own.

6

Let Go

Finding the Strength to Open Your Hands

∧∧∧∧

REMEMBER THOSE cable cars I told you about? There's more to the story.

My girlfriends and I were standing in line to take a ride on one of the Powell Street cable cars. The earlier fog had lifted, and the sun brushed the city in broad streaks of gold and cream, making San Francisco look like a postcard from somewhere on the far side of the world. Fat-bellied pigeons strutted around us, traversing memorized paths from the benches to the bohemian cafés. Standing there, my eyes moved from the glistening glass fronts of buildings down toward the cobblestones. That's when I saw it: two words, painted in huge white letters on the street.

"Let Go."

Sometimes the writing is on the wall, and sometimes it's on the ground beneath your feet.

On a cobblestone street in San Francisco, what was the meaning of this?

When I was sitting near the gripman later, I learned that the words "Let Go" are painted on the cobblestones as a reminder for the cable car gripmen to release the cable at a precise point on the ride. If the gripmen fail to let go at the right time, they could inflict serious damage to the cables. They could also harm the people riding because the cars would eventually be forced to a sudden stop.

For most of the journey, the gripmen have to hang on tight to the lever; but when the time is right, they must let go.

Unlike the gripmen, I haven't always read the signs. I've hung on longer than I should and held more than my hands were meant to hold. I wonder how much damage I've inflicted under the chronic assumption that there's something I can do about everything.

It's often in the little things that I demonstrate an unwillingness to let go. In parenting, for instance, my inner Devoter has sometimes "helped" my daughters with projects to assure their success, rather than letting them learn through their own mistakes. I should have let go instead.

But there have been bigger errors in judgment. In college, before I met the man who would become my husband, I was involved in an unhealthy dating relationship, believing I could change my boyfriend. For months, I didn't see the reality that I needed to let go. In my work life, my inner

Driver occasionally added more work than I could handle. I sacrificed rest, trying hard to make it all work the way I wanted. I needed to let go.

Let go.

Those two words are a way to live a life of radical trust in God. But I am still learning to actually and practically believe them in my heart.

I'm a hang-on-tight girl. If you're my friend, I'll stick with you to the bitter end. If you're my kid, I will never give up on you. I have been known to grip tight to what I love: my family and their futures; my comfort; my safety; my agendas and priorities; my opinions. I've often thought that the best way to love a person is to hold on for dear life.

I read once that surrender is what happens when God hands you a blank piece of paper with a space for you to sign your name at the bottom and then you hand it back to him to fill in as he wills. Talk about frightening!

I know that I've done otherwise: Instead of a blank piece of paper, I have given him long lists of instructions and deadlines.

As much strength as it takes to hang on, for a woman like me, it takes even more to let go. Letting go has always seemed—if I'm honest—dangerous.

Tell me I'm not the only one.

Like Pole-Vaulting across the Grand Canyon

Of everything I've ever held on to, my kids have been the hardest to let go.

Here's a telltale way to determine if a woman has control issues: Watch how she reacts when her kid gets a driver's license.

Last fall, Lydia got a permit that allowed her to drive to and from school at age fifteen. It was the teenage equivalent of legally handing a three-year-old a set of Ginsu knives and sending her to the backyard for the afternoon. Lydia is a great kid, intensely responsible. Another mother told me recently how much her kid loves participating in group projects with Lydia, and I don't think I have to tell you why. This girl lets nothing slide.

But I was still terrified to let her drive. Her overconfidence only compounded my fears. This was the girl who, at age eleven, declared that she was *quite* ready to take the wheel. She told me this as she sat on her beanbag chair in front of the TV with a Wii game controller in her hands. "See, Mom?" she said, as she maneuvered her Mario Kart car along a precarious route. "I'm gonna be awesome at driving a *real* car!" (Moments later, her animated car crashed into the guardrail on a tight turn and burst into flames.)

Then she moved from animated to actual. *Jesus of Nazareth, be near.*

It became clear early on that most of her driver's training would fall under the calm and steady guidance of her father. By a unanimous vote, our family committee wisely determined that I was not fit to be a driver's ed instructor. I only added more stress to the situation. This was due to my hyperattentive behavior, my insatiable desire to grab the wheel, and—at least once—my inappropriate use of language. If I was going to lose my salvation anywhere, it would be while sitting in the passenger seat of Lydia's car.

Each time Lydia grabbed her backpack and headed to her car, the most defective parts of my inner Devoter were triggered. If I could have, I would have run beside her car for the full trip from home to school, shouting orders along the way: "Is your seat belt properly fastened? Don't you dare text and drive! Turn your music down; it's a distraction. Use your signal! Yield the right of way. I love you!"

Realistic mother that I am, I understand that I can't forever go running alongside her car. Resourceful mother that I am, I discovered another way to ~~control~~ monitor the situation.

This is what I did to protect her. For the first two weeks of driving, I stood at her car door before she backed out of the garage, and we went through my checklist:

Seat belt. Check.

Mobile phone tucked away. Check.

Both hands on wheel. Check.

I told her I loved her approximately sixteen times, in case I didn't get another chance—like I was going to jinx something if I didn't say all the words I wanted to say. Then I jogged from the garage out to the front step of the house to watch her drive down our long driveway, which cuts through the cornfields and then up over the hill. I prayed with the fervency of Elijah for the safety of that child. When Lydia's car was no longer visible, I grabbed my iPhone and opened the Find My Friends app. I spent the next ten minutes hitting refresh every thirty seconds on the app, which tracks the location of your friends and family using GPS technology.

Each day Lydia would arrive safely at school, texting me with a single word: "Here."

Proud of my attentive parenting, I told one of my friends what I had been doing every morning. I shared how the Find My Friends app provided an abundance of information on the well-being of my little driver. If her Find My Friends beacon stopped moving, that was a sure sign that Lydia had ended up in the ditch. If her beacon moved too fast, she was probably in an ambulance, on her way to the emergency room.

"Oh, I get it," my friend responded in her native tongue, sarcasm. "I can see how effective that would be. Because when you're tracking her like that, you can actually *prevent* her from getting in an accident, right?"

Translation: "Help *me* help *you*, Jennifer. Put the phone *down*."

Sometimes the bravest thing a mother can do is put down the phone, the bottle of disinfectant, and the baby monitor. I'm not kidding when I tell you that the kids had monitors in their rooms until they were in kindergarten. The girls are teenagers, and I still occasionally sneak into their rooms to make sure they're breathing.

For me, letting go is about as easy as pole-vaulting across the Grand Canyon.

I used to think that bravery was hanging on when you

want to let go. Then I became a mom and found out that bravery is letting go when you want to hang on.

If we let go of the string, a helium balloon floats away. If we let go of the leash, the dog bolts. If we let go of the steering wheel, a car eventually veers off course. If we let go of the rope, we fall fast.

Letting go is hard, hard work, people, and I'm not intrinsically bent toward it. So often, letting go is visually represented as a woman walking through a pastoral field of wildflowers, silhouetted against the sun, with her hair flowing down her back. I only wish that surrender was that pretty and Instagram-worthy. But that's not reality, and I've resisted the urge to present surrender to you in that way. (In fact, when my publisher asked me what kind of image I preferred for this book cover, I said, "Anything but a woman walking through a field of wildflowers.")

Because how do you easily, breezily let go of the child growing up too fast? The wayward teen who barges out of the house, slamming the door behind him, spewing hateful words? The mounting debt and accumulation of bills? The hurt inflicted by an inattentive spouse? How do you let go of the friend who might never come to know the truth of Christ's teachings? How do you easily let go of fear when the doctor delivers the terminal diagnosis? How do you let go of the hurt?

How do you let go of your to-do list when it feels like you're the only one who can do it?

God tells us, "It's all under control." But in this crazy,

Bravery
*is letting go when you
want to hang on.*

crazy world, do you really want to let go and allow an unseen Being to prove himself?

I've had trouble letting go of far lesser things—like too-small jeans and silly grudges. My inclination is to try to hang on and fix the unfixable, and I don't always realize that my efforts are about as futile as rearranging deck chairs on the *Titanic*.

With each passing year, I've had to let go of more and more. Letting go always feels like I'm dangling on the edge of a cliff, fingernails digging into a rocky crevice.

In the quiet, if I listen to Jesus, I sense him speaking into my soul: *Trust me. I'll catch you.*

We will never know if we can trust Jesus if we don't give him the chance to prove it.

Friend, letting go isn't cowardly. It's so very courageous.

When the Old Methods Stop Working

How do we know when to hang on and when we need to just let go? I wish there were a formula for this. I wish that when we were driving along in life, God would spray-paint the road beneath us with the big words "Let Go," so we would know, like the gripman, when it was time.

One night after a prayer service at my country church, I stood at the back by the coats and the mailboxes. I had my car keys in hand and was about to leave, but I felt the urge to turn back. I needed to talk to a friend who is a few years older and wiser than I, the kind of woman who doesn't hold back. After everyone else was gone, she and I sat in two chairs, knee to knee, behind the back row of pews in our dimly lit church. Above us, the steeple rose toward the black-as-oil sky, pinpricked with the light of ten thousand stars.

I told my friend what I knew in theory: I had to let go of something.

"But I feel like I was programmed a different way, you know? I don't know how to let go, and frankly, I don't know if I *want* to because I don't know what will happen if I do. God has been showing me places where I need to let go, but I just don't understand how. I've been hanging on to everything for so long. I don't know any other way."

My friend made a poignant observation that went something like this: "Sometimes we want something so badly that we continue to employ the same methods over and over again, perhaps with slight adjustments, each time expecting the desired result. Sometimes God will ask you to do what you've been doing so faithfully all of these years. He sees you . . . how you keep trying, keep adjusting, how you keep standing back up when you don't think you can. That's what perseverance is, and God is so proud of you. But you have to look at what you're doing to yourself. At times, you keep banging your head against the wall, expecting a different result, and wondering why the bleeding won't stop."

In that moment, I realized that so many of my wounds were bleeding profusely. I had been banging my head against the wall in so many areas of my life—hoping for resolution to unresolved conflicts, for the workload to ease itself on its own. I kept pushing. Kept moving. I rarely stopped long enough to discern God's direction.

For much of life, quitting has seemed like a spiritual weakness. Any blood from my wounds was the price I had to pay to make the world better.

My friend and I sat quietly in the sanctuary, with the wooden cross nailed to the wall. *The cross.* Jesus literally drained himself of blood and life for us, the ultimate act of letting go. Jesus doesn't expect us to bleed ourselves dry from wounds for which he bled already.

I had to ask myself, *Do I truly trust the finished work of Christ? Do I truly trust that Jesus has my life under his control?*

There is a place where our fear has to meet God—and it's at the foot of the cross.

Fear of Intimacy

The night before Jesus went to the cross, he reclined at a table with his closest friends and offered words of comfort: "Do not let your hearts be troubled. You believe in God; believe also in me" (John 14:1).

That word "believe" is *pisteuete* in the original Greek. But pisteuete belief is more than being convinced of God's existence—so much more. Pisteuete belief means to "have trust in."

Disciples of Christ are called to a place of pisteuete: "Do not let your hearts be troubled," Jesus is telling us. "Pisteuete in me." Trust in me.

We are believers of Jesus, but are we *trusters* of him?

I don't think I have been, and my hands are trembling as I type this confession to you: I don't always trust God because I'm scared to.

My lack of trust in God is the reason I don't let go of what I want.

As I mentioned in an earlier chapter, my primary motivation for my all-hands-on-deck approach to life is a deep love for my people. I love my family and my work so fiercely that I run on all cylinders for them.

But I've also controlled out of a place of fear.

I have been scared to let go of so much in my life because I lack what it truly takes: trust in God. I'm afraid to give God control of what's in my hands because I'm afraid I won't like what he does with my life without my "helpful" input.

There's more to this confession.

I go overboard in planning so much of my life because it seems less scary than the alternative. The alternative is intimacy with God. The closer I get to God, the greater the chance that I'm going to recognize his voice. And when I recognize his voice, there's a greater possibility that I'm going to hear him speaking into my heart, and I might not like what he tells me. What if he asks me to let go of someone I love or compels me to apologize to someone I don't want to face? What if he asks me to take something off my calendar that I treasure, something that has become a part of my identity? I am afraid of who I am without some of those things.

I don't always want to hear what God says, so I keep my distance at times.

I was shocked when I first discovered this about myself. I was shocked by how I guarded every other area of my life like a hawk: my kids, my work priorities, my marriage. But I had not guarded my intimacy with God in the same way because I was afraid of getting too close. I feared what it would cost me if I let go and listened.

In the process of writing this book and asking you to take a self-inventory of your life, I've had to take a self-inventory of mine. I haven't always liked what I found.

I don't want to sound overly dramatic here, but there were times during the writing of this book when I needed to step away from the page because of what God was revealing to me.

Friend, you wouldn't trust me with a message that I've never had to live. I had to live this one. Big time. During those stretches away from the manuscript, I spent long overdue time with Jesus, developing a relationship of trust. This kind of full stop is a challenge for the practical, achieving type of person. So believe me, the things I'm asking you to do in this book, I've had to struggle through myself.

Yes, I was scared of what I'd hear when I spent time with Jesus. I was ready for his chastisement and admonishment for not trusting him like I should have. What I was not ready for was this: his tenderness.

One night I leaned back into my pillow, laced my fingers behind my head, and stared at the ceiling for a long time. I took a deep breath.

With every exhale, I let each burden in my life unhinge

itself from my soul and fly skyward, up through the ceiling. It was as if everything I loved was attached to a colorful balloon, flying high, out of sight. There were names and words on each of the balloons: My husband, Scott. My girls, Lydia and Anna. My parents. This book. An unresolved conflict with a friend. My future. My fears. Our country. There was so much pain and hurt written on those balloons. As I watched them drift away, I realized there were a few balloons I'd been holding on to since I was a little girl.

Up, up they went.

I realized what I was doing: I was letting go.

Suddenly I slammed my eyelids shut out of fear. This was a frightening exercise of faith.

Have you ever felt in your bones that verse about perfect love driving out fear?[1] I had read that verse hundreds of time, but that night, I really *felt* the words.

In that moment, I felt the love of Christ driving my fears away. I felt the "with-ness" of Jesus. With Jesus beside me, I could open my eyes again.

I need Jesus to be my Lord. I need Jesus to be my Savior. But that night, I really needed him to be my friend, sitting with me as I let go of all that I'd held so tight. In that moment, I remembered how my friend Janelle prayed for my father-in-law back in 2009 when he was on hospice. As she prayed, she said she imagined Jesus sitting cross-legged on Paul's bed.

That night, in my own bed, I needed Cross-Legged Jesus.

I allowed myself to imagine him in that way, sitting on the

bed with me, like a friend, while the coyotes howled in the windbreak of trees outside the window. If Jesus had spoken to me out loud that night, I imagine this is what he would have said: "I'll be with you as you do this, day after day after day, right up to the end of the age."[2]

He is with us as we do this. He is with us as we figure out how to let go—and how to hang on.

Let go of the balloons. Imagine Jesus sitting with you, cross-legged at the end of your bed, as you let each one go. And then look closer. Imagine him holding the strings to all the balloons. They aren't floating away. They are held steady in his hands.

For everything you've ever let go, Jesus is still hanging on.

The Spiritual Discipline of Active Trust

I've been carried this year to a place of "active trust."

My default is disbelief and distrust. That tendency has been evident not only in my spiritual life (for years I was an agnostic), but in my interpersonal relationships. During the first months I was dating Scott, for instance, I had a terrible time trusting him. What if he betrayed me? But the more time I spent with Scott, the more I loved him. The more I loved him, the more I wanted to know everything about him: his interests, his habits, and his favorite food, rock band, color, song, books, jokes, cities, movies, restaurants, sports, and more. I couldn't get enough.

The more I came to know Scott, the more I came to trust him. I learned during our dating years that you can't trust someone you don't know. The same principle applies to our relationship with God: You cannot trust someone you don't know.

Friend, perhaps you have been loving and serving Jesus for a while now. But how well do you *know* him? Can you let go of the balloons and trust that he's still holding them all in his hands? This is active trust. There's an old saying, "Fake it 'til you make it." Active trust is more like this: "Faith it 'til you make it." It's like giving yourself the gift of future faith, in advance.

I joked recently with a friend that God is constantly putting a giant sticky note on my heart with the words, "I know how this all turns out." It's not an actual sticky note, but you get the point. God knows my long history with unbelief, and he's heard my cry: "I do believe! Help my unbelief."[3]

God really does know how this all turns out. Maybe we'll have to wait until heaven to know he was trustworthy in all that is yet to unfold in our lives. But until then, we have a choice. We can choose to trust God anyway. We can choose active trust. We can trust him with all that we are because we believe he is all he says he is. He hasn't done all that we wanted, but he has done all that is right.

And right now, that is enough for me.

The Words on Your Balloons

What are the words written on your balloons?

Do you sense God urging you to let go of them?

You may need to let go of a few things that are bad for

you—an addiction, a bad habit, a relationship that is no longer healthy. You may need to let go of things that are quite good—such as a few obligations on your overcommitted calendar. You may need to let go of that deluded belief that if you worry about something enough, it will resolve itself. During the last year, I have had to let go of things I'd held on to for years. I had to let go of a friendship that had become toxic; a messy relationship that so burdened me it even invaded my dream life. Until I let go. I had to let go of opportunities to speak at some amazing conferences because I was stretched too thin and was missing life at home. I had to let go of wrong thinking that if I didn't rescue my kids, they'd never succeed.

I had to ask myself some hard questions: Am I hanging on because I'm afraid of what will happen if I don't? Am I hanging on because I don't trust God as much as I trust myself?

Sometimes God will ask us to let go of something because it's not good for us. Sometimes he'll ask us to let go of something to make room for what's better.

God is teaching me an important

What to Let Go Of

- ▸ Regret
- ▸ Shame
- ▸ Excuses
- ▸ Bad habits
- ▸ Addictions
- ▸ Judgments
- ▸ Lazy attitudes
- ▸ Your mistakes
- ▸ Excessive worry
- ▸ Toxic relationships
- ▸ Ungrateful thoughts
- ▸ Self-defeating self-talk
- ▸ Labels you've worn for years
- ▸ Your desire to impress people
- ▸ The notion that you've got to be right
- ▸ Your try-hard efforts to change others
- ▸ People who refuse to see the best in you

concept about letting go: When I let go of what's good, I make room for what's best.

When I let go as a mom and stop treating my daughters like infants, I allow them to grow into the beautiful, responsible women they were made to be.

When I let go of a toxic relationship, I make room in my heart for healthier friendships.

When I say no to some wonderful opportunities to speak, I have time to write this book.

What is God asking you to let go of?

Let go, even if it hurts.

Let go of your need to control what happens at church, and give someone else the opportunity to lead.

Let go of an addiction, and make room for what your heart is really longing for—more of Jesus.

Let go of the anger that consumes your thoughts to make room for the joy you were made for.

Let go of the bitterness toward the person who hurt you and give your soul permission to run free.

Like the gripman, we'll have to pay attention to the road we're traveling. Sometimes we'll have to hang on. And sometimes we'll have to let go.

Will you know which to choose? You will. You'll know in the way a friend speaks truth to you. You'll know in a moment of clarity from God. You'll know when you begin to taste the freedom that comes as you say the word *no*—only to discover that the world didn't fall apart after all.

Jesus will show you how. In fact, he already did just that.

Jesus voluntarily *let go* of his place in heaven, hurling himself down through space and time to save a world begging for life.

He did it for love.

Jesus Christ let go of heaven to *hang on to us.*

Cracking the Control Code ∿∿∿∿∿∿∿∿∿∿

If you're still not sure. Here's the question we all want the answer to: Should I hang on or let go? God generally doesn't spell it out on the cobblestones for us. But he does give us discerning hearts, his Scriptures, and trusted advisers as guides.

When it comes to deciding whether to take on or let go of requests and commitments that require investments of your time and expertise, the Decision Tree on page 265 can help you determine how to proceed. (Additional copies of this Decision Tree can be found at www.ItsAllUnderControlBook.com/Resources.) At the top, write the problem or decision you are facing, and then filter it through each stage. This tree will require you to stop, pray, and listen for God's leading at each step. You may also need to reassess decisions. If God does ask you to let go of something, that doesn't imply that the door has been forever slammed shut. Regular reevaluation may be in order.

Important note: This tool will help you with decisions such as whether to take on a commitment at church or work. This tool could help you decide whether to intervene in something with which your child is struggling. It could also help you decide how to respond to a relational conflict with a friend. This tool is not intended for use in making major, life-altering choices, like whether to file for divorce. In those cases, immediately seek trusted biblical counsel and God's guidance through his Word and prayer.

If you have to let go of something big. Letting go can be one of the hardest things we'll ever do. Often, we must resurrender someone or something repeatedly. In that case, sit before the Lord and imagine the person or thing you need to let go of sitting inside of your clenched fist. Now open your hand to God.

If the thing in your hand is something harmful or sinful—like a bad habit or addiction—write it on a piece of paper and burn it.

7

Switcheroo

Why Every Control Freak Needs to Take God Off Her To-Do List

∧∧∧∧

I'M ABOUT TO ASK you to do something that will sound absurd at first, so let me give you the backstory before we begin.

It was 2004—the year I fell in love with Jesus and embraced God's plan for my life. For years, every morning I'd wake up and chirp, "What are we doing today, Lord?"

I can tell you I have never once heard God speak audibly to me, but I knew he was speaking to my soul. Maybe this is how that "still small voice" works. I came to recognize that the voice had the dialect of Scripture, the cadence of a friend's trusted advice, the soothing tone of a song. Those right-timed messages led me to make decisions about career and family. Pre-Jesus, those messages seemed like coincidences, but I began to see them as "God-incidences." I was so taken with God-incidences, I wrote about them regularly on my blog.

In those days, I went about my life feeling like I was partnering with God rather than playing God. Since childhood, I'd been bent toward wanting to call the shots, but with great relief, I knew—at last—that it wasn't all on me. I wasn't in charge of outcomes. Even when everything went south, God kept my eyes true north. I kept waking up every morning, asking the Lord for his agenda, and I kept listening for the answer.

My old journals reveal what an impact that relationship of trust made on my life. The pages exhale peace, hope, and innocence. My faith—new as it was—profoundly shaped how I handled disappointments in my career, how I dealt with postpartum depression, how I responded to surprises. My faith was so childlike and so beautiful. Flipping through those old journal pages not long ago, I cried over the tenderness of my heart. I trusted him so much.

That relationship of trust, beautiful as it was, didn't happen on its own. It took work, time, and commitment—the spiritual discipline of active trust. My life proved true the verse in James: "Draw near to God, and he will draw near to you."[1] My waking hours were spent alongside Jesus—reading the Scriptures, talking with spiritual mentors, taking crazy risks that would prove God faithful after all. Recently a friend's daughter, now grown, told me that one of her first memories of me was when our two families were on a vacation at the lake. She watched through the crack of the bathroom door as I read the Bible while blow-drying my hair. I couldn't get enough of God.

But notice how I've written about all of this in the past tense. What happened?

I stopped doing what it took. It didn't happen overnight, but in a series of weeks that turned to months. It's the way some couples describe how a marriage can lose its spark. Over time, they drift apart. In my relationship with God, he didn't drift; I did.

To put it simply, I got really busy. That's not an excuse, but it's the reason. I knit myself to a variety of tasks instead of to God. I clearly had forgotten a sermon illustration I heard years ago—that one of the enemy's most effective strategies to distract humans from Jesus is to "keep them busy."

My weekly calendar—though just a piece of paper sitting on my desk—began to carry a heavier weight than my prayer journal. In the haze of productivity, the problem was unrecognizable at first. A nagging sense alerted me that something was missing, but it took another two years to figure it out. My appetite for agency over everything betrayed my deepest fears about my future. My lists and plans were a way of making sure I knew *exactly* what was coming in the days and months ahead. (And, yes, I realize how ridiculous this sort of life surveillance looks when it's all written out.)

You know the old saying about plans: "If you want to make God laugh, tell him your plans." You probably also know the even older saying: "We can make our plans, but the LORD determines our steps" (Proverbs 16:9, NLT).

When I finally waded through the fog and came out the other side, I realized how my ambition had carried me to a place I didn't want to be: far enough from God that I could find him at church but couldn't recognize his voice in my kitchen.

The battle for my heart was being waged on the pages of my to-do list. The tasks that beguiled my inner Driver were winning. So I did what I thought was the most reasonable and holy response: I put God on my to-do list. In fact, I put him at the very top of my to-do list. I literally wrote his name down—*G-O-D*—right next to a perfectly drawn check box on my memo pad.

Several books I'd read encouraged people to set aside specific times and places to draw away with the Lord. So I bought a thirty-dollar chair at a consignment shop and filled a basket with my favorite devotionals, three Bibles in different translations, a prayer journal, and highlighters. Some mornings I lit a candle. And for years, I met God there.

I sat in that assigned spot for my quiet time, next to a flickering vanilla-scented votive. After a while, something felt off, not at all like the way I'd felt during the two-year honeymoon after I renewed my commitment to Jesus. I knew I was in danger when I found myself looking at the clock during my minutes in that chair. Some days, if I didn't "get something out of my quiet time," I resented God. I didn't realize it then, but I often treated the God of the universe like an employee instead of my boss, telling him what I needed him to do in order for me to do what I needed to get done. I used to wake up asking, "What are we going to do today, Lord?" But a dangerous shift occurred: I began to come to him with a list of my demands.

The Savior of my life became an item on the list. "Spend fifteen minutes with Jesus." Check. Move on.

What a terrible way to grow the single most important and defining relationship of my life. I'm not saying there's anything wrong with quiet time. But I am saying that quiet time is ineffective if I leave Jesus at my living room chair and get so busy that I forget to partner with him the rest of my day.

I was so convicted recently by this Francis Chan illustration. He begins by describing a scenario familiar to parents everywhere—what happens when he tells his daughter, "Hey, go clean your room":

> She's not going to come back a couple hours later, and say, "Hey Dad, I memorized what you said to me. You said, 'Go clean your room.'" What am I going to say, "Oh good job! That's what I wanted!" No.
>
> And she's not going to come to me and say, "Dad, I can say 'Go clean your room' in Greek. Listen." That's not going to fly!
>
> And what if she said, "You know what? My friends and I, we're going to gather together and every week we're going to have a study, and we're

going to figure out what it would look like if I cleaned my room." No, none of that's going to fly. Just go and clean it. She knows that. So why do we think that this type of thinking or this type of talk is going to work with Jesus?[2]

I was reading God's Word. I was memorizing his Word. But I wasn't really breathing it in. Even when we're not blatantly disobeying God, we can treat time with him as a mouthed abstraction that isn't actually changing anything inside of us.

Looking back now, those hours in the chair often felt like visitation hours at the prison, when the guard gives you time to talk on an old-fashioned phone with a thick piece of cloudy glass between the two of you. You see the one you love on the other side, but you're not really touching—just pressing fingers to the cold glass. I was the prisoner.

My quiet time had lost effectiveness because I treated Jesus like an item on a list instead of Lord of my life. If I was going to live as if I truly believed God was in control, I had to learn to trust him again. I would never be able to surrender control of my life, my calendar, my to-dos, my children, and my marriage to someone I didn't trust.

The first step was this: I took God off my to-do list.

God's Got It

That's right. I took God off the list.

I watched my husband for cues on how to do this. For my

husband, a farmer, God isn't an item on the to-do list. God puts the list together and hands it to Scott every day.

God and Scott meet each morning in the living room over coffee and leather-bound Scripture. It's been like that for more than a decade, and Scott doesn't want you to think he's some super-Christian. Surrender, he says, came out of necessity, rather than some superpious gene he inherited. He is a farmer, always at the mercy of God.

I talk about that in my first book, *Love Idol*.

My husband can scratch back the dirt and drop tiny pearls from the planter, but he can't make the skies open. He can tug open stitched bags of designer seeds, but he can't cajole a green shoot from a pod. He can use GPS technology, but he can't prevent a hailstorm. He can mouse-click his way through forecasts all he wants to, but a snowstorm can still whip through his fields before the harvest ends.[3]

Scott, a man with strong Driver tendencies, can make all the plans he wants, but ultimately, the only plan that's going to work is the one God draws up for him. When my husband heads toward the pickup truck after morning coffee, Jesus goes out the door with him. Jesus isn't someone who hangs out in the living room, playing Candy Crush on his iPhone, waiting on the couch for Scott until tomorrow's quiet time.

This is, of course, true for all of us. Jesus goes with us to the supermarket, the dentist's office, the vet, the hair salon. But we aren't always aware in the same way that a farmer is aware. Farming is putting yourself in a position to trust God. It's a way of life in which you can't miss the truth: God is God of the clock, God of the calendar, God of the weather, God of the to-do list. God alone knows when the rain will come, when the heat will rise, when it's time for the seed to push up from the dark into the light.

A lot of people have romantic notions about farm life. But hard things lie beneath the idyllic overlay. There are grueling uncertainties, great losses, late nights, crazy markets, droughts, insects, disease, hailstorms, equipment that breaks down when you need it most, and tragically, despair that has led to a higher-than-average suicide rate nationally.[4]

Scott says he has no choice but to trust God. For years he's gone around this farm saying, "God's got it." And when he says, "God's got it," he is talking himself into the truth. That's a form of active trust.

In Western culture, it's tempting to say "God's got it" but not really live it. We're more of a "you got this" culture.

You want to pursue your passion? You got this.

You want to start a business? You got this.

You want to start a new exercise program? You got this.

You've definitely got it in you to do all of those things, but how often do you and I forget that what's "in us" *is the very Spirit of God*?

We live in a culture where we've set ourselves up to play God. The first time that I found out my mammogram was abnormal, my immediate instinct was to run for the Google machine and ask it what "asymmetrical tissue" means.

For almost every possible scenario, we have a means of control available to us: a spray to control weeds, a cream to control wrinkles, a pill to control hunger. It's no wonder we've been fooled into thinking we are the ones calling the shots. It's hard to surrender our lives to God when we've got everything covered ourselves, isn't it?

This, of course, leaves us feeling on the hook for everything. And suddenly we turn around, inspect our lives, and find that Jesus has become an item on our to-do lists.

What do we want with our lives? What do we really want? When we strip all the faux self-sufficiency away, we can see it clearly. We want Jesus. We are hungry for the God who first stole our hearts. We want to do the things that God wants us to do. We want to partner with him, not boss him around. When we lay our heads down at night, we want to feel the incomparable satisfaction of knowing we spent our day in the center of his will. We want to be remembered as women who did exactly what God wanted us to do—rather than as overworked, weary women who lost their joy.

Nothing else on *our* to-do lists matters as much as knowing we were completely obedient to *his*. Nothing will give us more joy than giving our yes when God invites us to be a part of what he's already doing.

Rather than bringing our agenda to God, we can be servants to the agenda that he has for us. He does not have to be an item on our to-do list anymore. Instead, we can start our day by handing him the list and letting him guide us in what to put on it.

We talk about how Christ is in us, which is totally true! But what if we saw the bigger truth: that we are in Christ? Here is a visual representation of that truth:

Christ in us

We are in Christ.

That same principle applies to our to-do list.

To-Do List
God
Laundry
Carpool
Vet
Wash car
Call insurance agent

Let's take God off our to-do list and hand the whole thing over to him. It's a strategic, spiritual switcheroo. God, who holds all things together,[5] can handle everything on your list, including what goes where. He is not one piece of the list; he's the holder of it.

Why settle for a piece of God, when you can have the whole peace of God?

Do Whatever He Tells You

Taking God off our to-do list will require a new way of thinking and responding.

Our mentor will be Mary, the mother of Jesus. Here's her advice: "Do whatever he tells you."[6]

Let's walk through the doors of the wedding in Cana. As you'll recall, this wedding is the site of Jesus' first miracle. He turned water to wine. One of the reasons I love this particular miracle is that it's proof that God cares about the little things. Jesus' first miracle wasn't a healing. That night, he didn't give someone their sight on the spot or command a paralyzed man to stand on his own two feet.

He made wine.

Yes, God cares about the big stuff of life: crops, cancer, and catastrophes. But he also cares about the little stuff, including everything on your to-do list, every single day. Friend, if it matters to you, it matters to God. Your deadline matters to God. Your yard work matters to God. Your sore throat matters to God. Your scuffle at the office matters to God. The spat you had with your husband last night matters to God.

The story at Cana is proof.

At the wedding reception, the servants discovered that the wine had run out. This would have been considered a major faux pas in first-century Galilee.

Jesus' mom was at the wedding, and I totally love how she responded. Unless she had been assigned the role of wedding planner, she really had no business interfering. I think she was a bit like you and me. She just wanted to help. Maybe she was a Devoter. Maybe she loved her friends so much that she wanted to spare them the embarrassment of running out of a key staple for the party.

She took decisive action, marched up to her son, and delivered the news: "They have no more wine."

Jesus responded, "Dear woman, that's not our problem" (John 2:3-4, NLT).

At that point, Mary could have taken matters into her own hands and headed to the market to buy the wine. But because she trusted Jesus, she spun toward the servants and said, "Do whatever he tells you" (verse 5).

Do whatever he tells you. This, my friend, is the original #FixItJesus.

Mary knew her son could fix this problem, but I doubt that she knew how. Maybe Mary thought he would point the servants to the nearest winery. Who knows what she imagined Jesus would do. At this point, it probably would have been crazier than a corkscrew for her to imagine that her son could perform a miracle of the magnitude he was about to perform. Because at this point, as far as Scripture tells us,

Biggest Pet Peeves of Control Freaks

- When people inexplicably fail to recognize the genius of your ideas

- When your husband cleans the bathroom wrong

- When you plan the day, and no one follows your script

- When the guy ahead of you in the supermarket express lane has thirty-two items, and you have the maximum ten

- The inability to finish the shampoo and conditioner bottles at the same time

- When you're on vacation but not in charge of the itinerary. Or worse, *there is no itinerary.*

- Being told to relax, chill out, or "don't stress." (Come a little closer and say that.)

no one in the room had seen what he was capable of—raising people from the dead, unstopping deaf ears, sending demonized pigs over cliffs, feeding large crowds of people at once.

So imagine the wild obedience it would have taken for those servants to do what Jesus told them to do next.

Jesus handed the servants their to-do list.

First up on the list: "Fill the jars with water."

So they filled them to the brim.

Second on the list: "Now draw some out and take it to the master of the banquet."

Imagine the wide-eyed disbelief of the servants. If I were one of those servants, I would have politely dismissed Jesus, slowly backing out of the room. "You know, um, thanks, Jesus. But I think I'll see if Trader Joe's has any Two Buck Chuck on the shelves."

Would I seriously consider pouring out water from huge jars used for ceremonial washing?

Not a chance.

But those servants did the unthinkable. First, they listened to Mary, who told them,

"Do whatever he tells you." And then they took Jesus' to-do list and carried out the tasks exactly as he assigned them.

"They did so, and the master of the banquet tasted the water that had been turned into wine. He did not realize where it had come from, though the servants who had drawn the water knew" (verses 8-9).

The master then called the bridegroom aside and congratulated him on serving such fine vintage. Sip, sip, hooray!

One of the coolest parts of the story is this: Because of this astounding water-to-wine miracle, "his disciples put their faith in him" (verse 11, CEV).

Imagine what our lives would be like if we let go of our lists and did whatever Jesus told us to do. Imagine who might put their faith in Jesus on account of our obedience to the list handed to us by the Master.

"Do whatever he tells you." Ask the Lord every day for your instructions.

"Do whatever he tells you." Say yes to the invitation to partner with him.

"Do whatever he tells you." No matter the task, the assignment, the deadline. Ask him to guide you, and then obey his commands.

"Do whatever he tells you." Become so intimately familiar with the voice of Jesus that you can recognize it. Then say yes to whatever crazy, wonderful, unexpected, wacky thing he's asking you to do.

You don't know what will come of your wild obedience, but Jesus does. He knows how to turn your water into wine.

If we continue to hold tightly to our own agendas—giving Jesus fifteen minutes at 7 a.m., then moving on—we will never know what could have been.

Do whatever he tells you.

We need those five words to guide our daily decisions. The world is a buffet of choices: which college, which church, which job, which friends. That's the big stuff of life.

But think of all the seemingly little decisions you make every day: which work tasks to undertake, which direction to go, which doctor to choose.

It can all feel terribly overwhelming, and I have so often been tempted to make choices that suit my interests rather than God's. I have spent too much time putting Jesus on my to-do list and calling it good.

Let's ask for *his* list instead.

Recently I put this new plan in place. I started praying a simple prayer every day—a way of seeking God's guidance first. I don't always get it right, but praying this prayer keeps my heart aligned with his. The prayer is this: "God, help me to make choices today that honor your plans for my life."

I know. Easy words to say. Harder words to live by.

But when I think back to my honeymoon years with God, I remember that this is possible. I'm in the process of hearing God speak again.

I pray today that we will always remember that God's plans are bigger than ours—which means that the fruit of our choices might outlive us.

As we step into all that God has for us, let's respond wholeheartedly to the command "Do whatever he tells you."

Jesus is not an item on your to-do list. He is holding the list. And when you partner with him, you will be invited to take part in the amazing work he is already doing.

Maybe you wonder how you'll know. I promise you. You will. Set aside the list for a moment. Simply pray: "Dear God, never let me be so busy that I can't hear your voice."

Cracking the Control Code /\/\/\/\/\/\/\/\/\/\/\

For the next week, make it a point to practice taking God off your to-do list. Plan every day as if God were sitting next to you while you put together your daily agenda. As you sit with him at the kitchen table or your desk, tune in to God's agenda for your day. Consider making this exercise a part of your regular morning prayer time. (If you don't have a regular morning time, how about starting one today?)

And then "do whatever he tells you." As you put your list together, don't expect to hear a booming voice from heaven. *Do* expect moments of discernment, sharpened with regular practice. This activity will help you see that all you do in a day is a way of partnering with God. "Whatever you do, do it all for the glory of God" (1 Corinthians 10:31).

If, in the course of your busy day, it's hard for you to remember that you are on God's agenda, draw a large circle around your to-do list and label the circle "GOD" as a reminder that this is God's list, not your own.

8

Clueless

What to Do When God's To-Do List Makes Zero Sense

∿∿∿∿

REMEMBER THE TO-DO LIST you made in consultation with God? I forgot to tell you something. There are times when the items on your list will make zero sense to you.

Ask me how I know.

Several years ago, a moms' group in California asked me to deliver a message about letting go of our need for people's approval. They wanted me to deliver that message via Skype instead of flying me from Iowa to California.

I said yes because I felt the Lord leading me to deliver this message, even though the medium was awkward. I also know the kind of pressure moms put on themselves to have it all together, and I believed my message would offer relief. (Good grief, we moms can be so aggressively awful to ourselves.) I saw this as an opportunity to apply a little word salve to their wounds.

We "met" on a weekday morning. I sat in my office in Iowa, in front of my bookshelves, the ones where all the books are arranged by color in rainbow order. (Surely these color-coded shelves don't surprise you.) I delivered my message through the laptop. As I spoke, my face and voice were projected, live, onto a giant screen at Menlo Church in Mountain View, California.

After I waved good-bye, I ended the Skype call and then promptly called my husband. This is what I said, while stomping around the house like a raving lunatic: "I am never, ever, ever, *ever* doing that again. That was awful! Horrible! Promise me you'll never let me do something like that again."

Here's why I freaked: The entire time I was speaking, I couldn't hear anyone on the other end. Nor could I see their faces. Because of the way the technology worked in the church's meeting room, the moms could see and hear *me* loud and clear on the screen. But I heard nothing—not even crickets. My view was a grainy video of the backs of heads.

I can't begin to tell you how difficult it is to speak to a crowd when you have no clue if the message is connecting. This is a control freak's worst nightmare.

The only real movement I saw in the room was this: women getting up to leave. Where were they going? What had I said? The assumption: *I am failing. My message is missing the mark!* (As Ursula famously said, "Don't underestimate the importance of body language.")[1]

Miraculously, I held it together for the full forty-five minutes, clinging to God like he was the last floating piece of wood after the *Titanic* sank. Inside of me, I knew this ship had sunk, and I felt like I had been tricked by God into saying yes to a digital voyage to California.

A few hours after the event, the organizer sent a kind e-mail, telling me how the women were impacted. I didn't believe her. Nope. I couldn't shake the feeling that I had bombed. I trusted my eyes and my ears more than I trusted her e-mail, more than I trusted my heart—*more than I trusted God.* I trusted my worst assumptions more than I trusted promises like "he who calls you is faithful" (1 Thessalonians 5:24, NLT).

The avalanche of negative self-talk was so deafening that I couldn't hear the voice of God. Plus, I can be kind of a know-it-all, so I already knew what God would tell me:

"Even if you only touched one person, it was worth it."

"You plant the seeds, and I will grow them."

Places That Will Unleash Your Inner Control Freak

- A friend's disheveled bookshelf—not arranged alphabetically, by size, color, or even by genre!
- Your kitchen, when you decide to let your child "help" you with a baking project
- In the parking lot where one car takes up two spaces
- The grocery checkout line managed by a teenage trainee
- At a red light, when you're behind someone who's on their phone and misses the light change—and then you have to feel guilty for honking
- At your computer, on a deadline, when the color wheel on your Mac won't stop spinning

"You are in charge of obedience; I am in charge of results."

"Trust in me, and lean not on your own understanding."

I already had in my mind what "success" would have looked like. I had read speaker-training courses that teach you to imagine yourself on stage, engaging with the audience. In this mental role-playing, the people are smiling at me. They aren't standing up and *walking away*.

After a few days of sulking in my failure, I repented of my unwillingness to listen to God. One morning, I took time to actually hear him out. I realized that my lack of trust ran deeper than this speaking engagement. My trust issues were why I had been prone to issues of control for most of my life. As I mentioned in chapter 6, the reason I want to handle parts of my life is because I'm afraid God won't come through. I'm afraid that I need to be in charge of all the outcomes, the safety nets, the contingency plans, and the escape routes at the zoo in the unlikely event of escaped lions, or worse, snakes. I will tell you that I trust God, but I don't always act like it.

As I explored my issues with control, deep down I became convicted that my trust is so small because I've made so much of my life about *my* agenda instead of God's. I'm scared to be completely obedient because if I don't take matters into my own hands, maybe I'll be disappointed with the outcomes.

Because let's face it: God's way is not always the path of least resistance. When we truly hand over the results to God, we might not like what happens. No wonder we relegate God to an item on the list! He looks safer when confined to a fifteen-minute slot at the beginning of the day and a few sweet prayers at the dinner table and again at bedtime. Boxed-up God feels tidy.

Maybe you've felt the same way. Think about a time you've done the obedient thing, walked a road God asked you to walk, and then felt the disappointment of finding yourself on an entirely different route than you expected. I have encountered far more crushing disappointments than that forty-five-minute Skype call with the women in California. So have you. Some of you took a new job, only to lose that job a year later in a massive layoff. Some of you dropped everything safe to enter the mission field. Then, despite your obedience, you entered into a spiritual crisis triggered by the suffering around you. You might feel like you're doing exactly what God asked you to do, but you never get a chance to experience the fruit of your efforts. In fact, you might not bear witness to the fruit during your entire time on earth. That's wild, scary obedience.

Perhaps that's how Moses felt. With courage and sweat on his brow, Moses led his people for forty years to the Promised Land. But he never stepped foot in it. At the end of his life, Moses stood at the top of Mount Nebo, overlooking the Promised Land. He could practically throw a rock and have it plop down on the culmination of his life's greatest assignment. But there he stood—an old man—on the outside of all that he'd worked toward, with God's hand holding him back. God spoke these words to him: "I have let you see it with your eyes, but you will not cross over into it."[2]

You will not cross over into it.

Think of times when you've done what you were called to do, yet the grand finale never played out. There was no roar of the crowd, no angelic choir singing overhead. The Promised Land stretched out before you while you stood frozen in the debris of your toilsome work, held back by the hand of God. *You will not cross over into it.*

You raised your kids, obediently training them up in the way a child should go, only to watch them make painful choices from which you wanted to rescue them. *You will not cross over into it.*

You listened to a sermon and felt convicted to ask for forgiveness from a friend. You gathered up courage to approach her, but she didn't accept the apology. *You will not cross over into it.*

You quit your job and felt called to move to the other side of the country, yet your extended family thought you were crazy. (If that's you, just remember: Jesus' family thought he was "out of his mind" too.)[3] You know you did what you were summoned to do, but you carry the disapproval of everyone else, and it breaks your heart. The Darling segment of your personality wants their stamp of approval, but *you will not cross over into it.*

Obedience is not for wimps. At first, obedience can resemble the passive posture of letting God carry you where he will. It turns out that obedience is quite often a gutsy thing that will compel you to stand upright and march forward, even if it threatens your security, your own longings, and your idea of success. Obedience is not an act of the weak, but a rising up of the strong. Obedience might embarrass you or inconvenience you. Sometimes it will leave you in the dark, and the only light you will see is the small patch pooling at your feet. You ask for a spotlight to see straight ahead into the next two years of your life, but instead God gives you a "lamp unto [your] feet"[4] and lets you see no further than this hour.

A voice deep within tells you, "It's all under control," but it's hard to believe that voice without visible results as hard evidence.

That morning when I repented—after the Skype event— I asked God to shine that lamp as far as he would let me see. I sensed God telling me this: *Long before you were born, I saw the big picture of everything. I assigned a few pieces for you to place during your time on earth. I am inviting you to set your pieces where they go and trust that I alone can see how they fit with the whole.*

Every day we have a choice to make. We can choose to believe that God sees a bigger picture and that we are here to put certain pieces in place, even when it doesn't make sense. Even when it's inconvenient. Even when it hurts. Even when we have to surrender every outcome.

There's nothing passive about surrender like this. Darlings must surrender approval ratings and reputations. Drivers must surrender their idealistic visions. Devoters must keep planting seeds of love, trusting God is working under the soil.

We Seriously Have No Clue

We really have no clue what God is up to. We think we do, but we don't.

It was a warm day in May. Location: the Sioux Falls, South Dakota, airport, where I was about to fly to Menlo Church in California. Yep. *Same church.* Had they forgotten about the Great Ministry Disaster from three years earlier? Maybe they believed in the grace of second chances.

I sat near a long bank of airport windows with my carry-on bag at my feet, a neck pillow on my lap, an open bag of almonds in my right hand. Other passengers had begun to line up, tickets in hand. I stared outside, asking questions of myself like: *Can you believe they're actually paying good money to fly you out there? What if you fail again?*

But the God-hearted part of me just said: *Shhhhhhhh. Peace. Be still.*

I flew to California. The next morning, I walked into a large room with round tables decorated in vibrant spring colors. At the front of the room, I saw the screen where my face had been projected three years earlier. Fear and embarrassment crept along my skin, making it feel prickly. Right then, a woman tapped me on the shoulder and enfolded me in a tight embrace. "I'm a hugger," she said. "I hope that's okay." I was welcomed like an old friend. Like a sister.

My time to speak came. I stood in front of 150 moms and delivered a message, my voice shaking a little at first. But my voice evened out, and I mustered confidence from a hidden place behind my heart. This time, it was different, so different. Unlike the Skype call, I could look into actual eyeballs and hear actual laughter and watch women wipe away actual tears. The message was connecting!

During my talk, I watched as women left their seats—just as I had seen them do three years earlier during my Skype visit. But now I could see why they were standing up and walking away: They were heading to the back of the room to bounce their crying infants!

Afterward I hugged dozens of mamas, listened to their struggles, shared in their joys, and cooed over their babies. Then two moms came up and said that they needed to talk to me. They had heard me speak during that Skype session.

Uh-oh, I told myself. *Brace yourself. This isn't going to be pretty.*

And then they told me about what had happened in their hearts that day. How it was just what they needed to hear. How someone at their table eventually became a follower of Christ. I was floored.

Please hear me—I'm not trying to make myself out as some gospel hero. I am telling you this story because of what I learned: We seriously have no clue. We really don't. We have no clue what God is doing in places we cannot see. We have no clue what happens to so many of the seeds we plant. We have no clue what God intends when we let him control our to-do list.

We are clueless.

That day, I learned that I can't always trust my eyes or my

ears. Some days I can't even trust my own heart. But I can always trust his.

There are times when obedience makes little sense. We won't understand what God is doing or how he is working—or if he is even there.

Just go with it. Handing over control to God is an invitation to cluelessness. Do not fear it: That's where the story gets really good.

"Lord, If You Had Been There"

Clueless.

That must have been how Lazarus's friends felt when Jesus didn't show up in time to heal him. Jesus had gotten word that Lazarus was ill, but oddly, he stayed where he was for two more days—long enough for Lazarus to die.

Meanwhile, many Jews came to comfort Mary and Martha.

When Jesus finally showed up, they must have wondered why he'd tarried. They must have been utterly clueless. Martha even met Jesus outside of the house. You can sense the anguish in Mary's voice when she says, "Lord, if you had been here, my brother would not have died" (John 11:32).

Pause the story here for a moment and think about the times when God seemed absent from your life.

How often have you felt this way? "Lord, if you had been here, _____ would not have died."

How do you fill in the blank? My reputation would not have died. My loved one would not have died. My dreams, my expectations, the outcome I wanted would not have died.

Mary and Martha had been obedient. They had welcomed Jesus into their home, had answered the call to be servants, and had been a part of his ministry. I think it's safe to say that spending time with Jesus was more than an item on their to-do list.

Now they had asked for *one thing*, for heaven's sake, and it looked like Jesus was a no-show.

"Lord, if you had been here, _____ would not have died." Like us, they really had no clue.

Jesus showed up four days "late." He called for the stone to be removed from the tomb. Martha warned him that the stench was going to be pretty bad.

Jesus responded: "Didn't I tell you that if you believed, you would see the glory of God?" (John 11:40, MSG).

So they removed the stone. Jesus shouted, "Lazarus, come out!"

Out Lazarus came, wrapped head to toe. Alive!

Four days late turned out to be right on time.

The story is significant for many reasons, but one reason in particular stands out. Remember all the Jews who had come to console Mary and Martha? They were standing there, jaws dropping, when Jesus raised a man from the dead. That moment was a turning point for many of the bystanders. They saw what Jesus did, in his perfect timing, and they believed in him because of it.

If Jesus had shown up on Martha's schedule, Lazarus wouldn't have died. But because Jesus didn't come "on time,"

Lazarus *did* die. That meant that Jesus could perform a miracle that resulted in the conversion of many Jews.

"That was a turnaround for many of the Jews who were with Mary. They saw what Jesus did, and believed in him" (John 11:45, MSG).

We long to be obedient to God, don't we? We long to give him the room to move according to his timetable. Yet we've been scared to give him access to parts of our lives because we're afraid he won't come through.

When we doubt, here's what we can remember: God's plan is bigger than ours. When Jesus resurrects the Lazaruses in our lives, perhaps there will be onlookers. Perhaps they will see what Jesus did, and they will believe in him too.

There are real people, real souls, waiting on the other side of your obedience.

Holy Spirit, Come

What has God called you to do? You may have to wait days, weeks, or even years to see the fruit of your obedience. As time passes, you may think God is a no-show. But when God is years late according to *your* calendar, he is right on time according to *his*.

For every one thing you do, God is doing another thousand things behind it. Your job is the one thing he stuck on your list. That's it. The one thing. The rest? For now, you have no clue.

God gave me a sweet gift that day in California—a chance to see the faces. Before I'd seen only faint, grainy shadows on a computer screen. That was a rare gift. Obedience does not always offer such gratification. Instead, obedience requires an eternal perspective because we may never see the results here on earth. There are times when we may have to wait all the way to heaven to know why God called us to be wildly obedient to weird and wonderful things.

When frustration comes, remember this: The most important work you ever do might outlive you.

Where do you need that kind of faith today—the kind of faith that will have you patiently waiting for heaven's big screen to watch the final scene of a story you were a part of?

Where do you need to be obedient today? What words have you spoken that you feel have fallen on deaf ears? What hope have you offered with no evidence of fruit? What fervent prayers keep you up at night? What feels like a failure? What can you not see today? Do you hear only silence? Is your own Lazarus still in the tomb?

Wait. Be still.

Invite the Holy Spirit: *Come.*

That's a dangerous invitation, isn't it? The Holy Spirit feels wild and . . . frankly, a little out of control. But that's who's been pestering you lately. That's who's been calling you into a life of wild obedience. That's who's got you covered when you're clueless.

When I pray, I generally direct my words toward God or Jesus. On this journey of surrender, I started praying to the Holy Spirit more directly in hopes that I would become more familiar with the person in the Trinity whom I too often ignore. One morning recently, I cried out to the Holy Spirit to be fire and wind and power in my life. I confessed how I often ignore him. I confessed how I go my own way, trusting my power more than his. (Yes, I realize how awful that sounds.)

When I prayed to the Holy Spirit that day, I felt his love for me. I felt his comfort and a firm sense that he has it all under control. His goodness moved me so thoroughly that I posted the entire prayer to Facebook that morning. I was pretty sure I wasn't the only one who needed to pray those words. Thousands of people read that prayer over the next couple of days and shared it on their own Facebook walls. Many reached out to me, saying they wanted more of God's power in their lives too. They wanted to be obedient, even if it meant they were clueless.

As we close this chapter, let's pray that prayer together.

Dear Holy Spirit,

I don't always pray to you. Maybe it's because you're harder to wrap my mind around. I "get" a Father. I relate to the person of Jesus. But, Holy Spirit, you are wind and wandering and wild. You are breath. You come and go as you please, and sometimes you light upon my skin like a flame. You are presence, and you are power. I look back on my life and see startling evidence of your fingerprints; those are always the weak-kneed moments that make me go, "Whoa."

You were present at Creation, hovering over the

waters, and you haven't left us since. You come to us through water and Word, bread and wine. I find you at the altar—and on the floor. I find you in my deepest joys and lingering around the edges of my heart when the pain is too much.

You kind of scare me because you remind me that my self-sufficiency is worth nothing when you're around. You like me weak, and I don't do weak well. You like me needy, and I don't do needy well. You never once let me be the hero. I am always the rescued. You are the helper, the counselor, the reassuring hand upon my back when I would have sworn to you that I was the only one in the room. When I neglect you, I'm like a candle without a flame.

You don't just bring the fire. You are the fire. You cause me to jump when I want to hide. You make me to run free when I want to walk away.

Holy Spirit, don't let me ever take another step in this life without checking in with you first—and surrendering myself wholly to you.

Holy Spirit, you are welcome here. Amen.[5]

Friend, let's believe it together: The Holy Spirit is working in the silences.

We really don't have a clue.

Our main job is not to manage outcomes. It is simply to show up. Everything else is up to God. We cannot always see "everything else." But someday, I believe, we will.

Cracking the Control Code ∧∧∧∧∧∧∧∧∧∧∧

Unconditional obedience. What is Jesus telling you to do that requires obedience without the guarantee of desired results?

Ask God to shine the lamplight on areas where he wants to stretch you in your obedience. Consider your work, parenting, marriage, ministry, and friendships. Then, over the next week, make a list as those areas are revealed to you. Commit to releasing your own control and giving them over to God in obedience.

Your acts of obedience don't have to be big. Every day is an opportunity to test out your obedience. With every yes, you are building trust.

You will never know what you are capable of doing if you don't say yes. Nor will you know what he is capable of if you don't pass the baton to him. This is the partnership of wild obedience.

It's why a man built an ark. Why a young boy took stones and a sling to face a giant. Why a young woman approached a king in his throne room on behalf of her people. What is he calling you to do?

Unconditional surrender. In what part of your life do you wonder what God is up to? Where do you feel discouraged, weary, or uncertain, even though you are doing what you feel God has asked you to do? What questions and outcomes do you need to surrender to the Lord? As you consider your answers, I invite you to pray that you will remember God's plans are bigger than yours:

Dear God, help us know that we might not see "results" in our lifetime, even when we are obedient. What looks like failure to us might look like obedience to you. We have handed our agendas and our to-do lists to you. Guide us to whatever you want us to do. Help us understand that some of what you're calling us to do might outlive us. We surrender our lives to you. Amen.

9

Room

It's Time to "Do, Delegate, or Dismiss"

LAST FALL I SIGNED UP for a home-decorating course. This was unusual for me because I live in a state of what I call Decor Denial. I haven't redecorated or repainted since we moved into our new home in 2002. Because I don't want to know what I'm missing, I generally avoid home-decorating blogs, *Better Homes & Gardens*, Parade of Homes tours, and the like. In short, I live in blissful ignorance to the out-of-date nature of my surroundings.

To clarify, we're not talking orange shag carpet and pink toilets here. But I knew that at the very least, our living room could use a fresh coat of paint. So I signed up for an online course called The Cozy Minimalist, led by Myquillyn Smith.[1] I took the course partly because I adore Myquillyn, and partly because she assured me that I wouldn't have to buy a bunch of new stuff to freshen up my house.

Our first assignment: Select one area and then "quiet the room." I picked our living room.

When you quiet a room, you take everything out of it except the essentials. Myquillyn says, "A quiet space exposes truth." It helps you get rid of what makes your room feel overstuffed, loud, and jumbled. And then after a time, you return the pieces that you truly love.

It took me nearly a half hour to unjumble my room. Why, you ask? Because I had collected fourteen years' worth of knickknacks and enough fake greenery to fill an aisle at Hobby Lobby. Our living room had become overrun with things I loved. I stripped the room and piled everything in our guest bedroom, where my beloved tchotchkes would wait until I decided what to put back. Most of the items in the pile were actually *good*, and many of them were meaningful. But sometimes you can simply have too much of a good thing.

After I finished quieting the room, I went back and admired the beautiful space that remained. Rather than feeling empty, our living room felt calm, rested, at ease, and unburdened.

I could breathe.

The Un-Quieted Rooms of Your Soul

I snapped a few photos of the room to share with the other Cozy Minimalists in our Facebook group. That's when I felt a lump of emotion rise up in my throat. The room had become an accidental metaphor for the human tendency to live an overstuffed, jumbled, noisy life. "A quiet space exposes truth." Isn't that what Myquillyn had said?

We so often fill our days with good things, *meaningful* things. We can generally handle a lot of tasks at once—*until we can't*. Quite often, we reach the point of "can't." Our souls' interior rooms can become like my living room.

For my part, I fill life with many things, most of them good. Yet in the same way that I lived in a state of Decor Denial, I live in a state of Duty Denial. I add more to my calendar because I buy into the idea that:

- I'm capable, therefore I should.
- It's the right thing to do.
- If I don't do it, no one else will.
- If someone else does it, it won't be done properly.

What, then, is the answer? And where do we begin?

The overstuffed nature of my living room wasn't obvious until I took all the items out. I then assigned them to one of three piles: keep, sell/give away, or toss. And then I asked myself the following questions:

1. What do I love?
2. What is essential?
3. What am I willing to give up?
4. What is good but no longer right for this room?
5. What simply needs to be discarded?

Right away, I could identify what I loved most: photos of our daughters, an antique clock from my great-grandmother, a glass fish that—while dated—is precious to me because it was a wedding gift from a special friend. Plus I think it's cute.

There were also items I didn't love, like my couch, but deemed essential because we didn't feel like we were in a position to purchase a new couch.

After quieting my room, I wondered, *Can I do the same thing with my life? Can I quiet my life?* I quickly realized that this exercise did translate easily to life. I needed a quieted life to expose the truth about myself. Until I took everything out and set it in front of me, I'd never know what to keep or toss.

So I brought my life to a hard stop. I needed to empty the rooms of my soul, reevaluate everything on my list, and just say no for a while. Professionally speaking, the timing was way off. Slowing down in this business when you're supposed to ramp it up can be tantamount to professional suicide. But for a season, I said no to endorsing other people's books, no to new speaking engagements, and more.

Standing along the quiet shore of my life as the tide rolled out, I was often moved to tears. I felt the same way that I'd felt while standing on the edge of my quieted room. I realized how addicted to hustle I had become and how culture uses busyness as a measure of worth. I confronted my inability to say no, my constant availability to everyone via text and Facebook Messenger, and the general overstuffing of my calendar.

I felt the sense of calm that I had been missing. My soul

had been properly quieted, and at last, I could hear God speaking into my life.

Answers to these questions began to emerge:

If I'm doing so much for others, why do I feel so distant *from* them?

If I'm so busy, why am I not more productive?

During my hard stop, it became clear that I often entered into a state of overcontrol, when I tried to shoehorn one more activity into my already-loaded schedule. My motives were generally good. So much of my doing was aimed at helping people I loved, but oddly, I was alienating them. In the foggy atmosphere of busyness, I no longer had time to truly connect on a meaningful level.

Maya Angelou is credited with saying, "I've learned that people will forget what you said, people will forget what you did, but people will never forget how you made them feel." I worried how I made people feel. During that hard stop, I discovered this essential truth: You can't control and connect at the same time.

So before adding anything back to my calendar and my life, I needed to ask myself those same five questions that I asked about my living room:

1. What do I love?
2. What is essential?
3. What am I willing to give up?
4. What is good but no longer right?
5. What simply needs to be discarded?

*Let go of
what God has not
asked you to do,
so you can shine
at what he has.*

Only when we answer those questions with intentionality; only when we can start saying yes to the best things and no to some good things; only when we can stop having to do it all; only then will we be able to live a life quiet enough to hear the voice of God.

My friend Suzanne told me once that she reevaluates her life in this way about every six months. She places everything on her list in front of God in prayer. Everything. "I've learned that if I invite God into the process, he'll show me what needs to be there and what doesn't."

After one such evaluation, she felt God leading her to take a sabbatical for a year from the Proverbs 31 speaking team. She wrote about the decision on her blog: "For a few weeks I privately went through a season of mourning. . . . I miss speaking, but my forever role is to simply love and follow Jesus. *In every season.* In everything that we do. If we hold on to something just because we think it's ours forever—we may stay long after it's time to release it."[2]

Perhaps you feel the need to release something too. Start by "quieting" your life.

Do. Delegate. Dismiss.

Imagine taking your whole life and setting it before you. Now take the time to evaluate every piece of it, like I did with the pile of my living room decor.

Take stock of it all: your family responsibilities, your household chores, your work assignments, your calendar, your studies, your exercise program, your date nights, your travel, your recreation.

Now pick up each piece and ask yourself questions about what you love and what's essential. Be honest with yourself: Can someone else help you with all that is on your plate? Do some of the things in your life simply need to be discarded?

As I mentioned, each item that made up my living room decor ended up in one of three piles: keep, sell/give away, or toss. I kept the best things, took a trunk full of decor to a consignment shop, donated some items, and tossed others.

You can employ a similar approach with your life evaluation. As you examine each piece of your life, set it in one of three piles marked do, delegate, or dismiss.

Do: These are assignments that you consider essential or that you simply enjoy.

Delegate: These are assignments that you will turn over to someone else. (I know how hard this is, so I've devoted the entirety of chapter 10 to the topic of asking for help.)

Dismiss: These are assignments that you will have to let go of, without guilt.

One thing I'm learning as I go through this kind of analysis is that I can't delegate or dismiss simply because I hate something. I don't particularly love my couch, but I have to keep it for now. I don't like tracking business expenses, but it's a part of the job.

I'm also learning how much easier it is to make choices if I have a clear understanding of my core values and boundaries. For instance, I am very unlikely to accept a speaking event if it conflicts with a major school activity. I rarely work past 4:30 p.m., even though my office is in our home. If assignments conflict with my core values, I say no. Lisa Whittle recently shared an Instagram post that perfectly describes how I feel about the importance of establishing core values and boundaries, especially as they relate to family: "My dreams had to be His dreams for me, lest I chased off into the sunset after some crazy cool thing my kids grew up to resent. . . . Jesus will never ask any of us to do things to hurt the structure of an institution He ordained."[3]

In this chapter's "Cracking the Control Code" section, I have included a helpful tool that will guide you through the process of "do, delegate, or dismiss."

But before we get there, let's pause and acknowledge what scares us most about this process.

When You Dismiss, You Will Disappoint

What are we really scared to do here? Put something in the dismiss pile, that's what.

The uncomfortable truth is this: When we say no, we will disappoint people. There's no way around it.

The belief that you've disappointed someone feels shameful. We pile more on because our sense of duty convinces us that we owe it to everyone to keep pushing. We can't imagine a world in which we aren't meeting and exceeding everyone's expectations.

Listen up. Jesus disappointed people too. He didn't stick around when people wanted him to stay and heal (see Mark 1:36-38.) He disappointed religious leaders when he dined with sinners (see Mark 2:16.) He aggravated people when he showed up "late" (see John 11:21).

You will disappoint people too. In time, you will be able to let go of the shame and offer a guilt-free no.

Here are a few steps toward dismissing what you need to let go without picking up the baggage of guilt:

1. **Know who you are.** It's tempting to tie your worth to your ability to get things done. But women with a clear sense of purpose and identity in Christ are able to say no without letting it prescribe something about their worth. Take time every day to affirm your truest identity—the one you have in Jesus.

2. **Know your priorities.** The clearer your priorities, the easier your decisions. Filter every request for your time through the prism of your core boundaries, values, and calling. If it doesn't pass the core boundaries test, it's a huge sign that you should dismiss it.

3. **Be resolute.** Sure, it's polite to offer an explanation for your no, but don't feel like you have to give a drawn-out justification, even if you know that your no will disappoint the asker. As Jesus said, "All you need to say is simply 'Yes' or 'No'" (Matthew 5:37).

4. **Keep perspective.** Remember that a yes to one more thing means a no to something else.

5. **Remind yourself that your no is someone else's yes.** Your no may open the door for another soul to learn, lead, and serve.

6. **Hear God's big yes over you.** There is wisdom in knowing when to walk away, and you will need courage to follow through. Know that when you need to say no, God is still in your corner, pouring all kinds of yes down on you! Hear these words from Paul: "Whatever God has promised gets stamped with the Yes of Jesus. . . . God affirms us, making us a sure thing in Christ, putting his Yes within us" (2 Corinthians 1:20-22, MSG).

One way to muster up the courage to say no is to practice on strangers or people you don't know very well. Reporter Kristin Wong offers one idea:

Practice being more aggressive when the stakes are low. For example, when a cashier asks you to sign up for a store credit card you don't want, try saying, "I don't use store credit cards" instead of a passive "Not today, but thank you," which implies your decision is up for debate.

It's a lot easier to be assertive with a stranger selling you something than it is when, say, your pleading coworker asks for a ride to the airport. Get comfortable with your assertiveness when it's easy so you'll be prepared when there's more pressure.[4]

You will find freedom in establishing ground rules for yourself, knowing what you simply won't do. That begins by extracting yourself from excessive commitments today.

Don't worry. You will still get to say yes to a lot of wonderful opportunities, designed by God specifically for you. And no doubt, God is going to ask you to do hard things and take on commitments that seem difficult. But he will not burden you to the point of breakdown.

This is the way we will get back to God's agenda for us: Do. Delegate. Dismiss.

You get to control your agenda. Don't let your agenda control you. It's time to figure out what doesn't matter, so you can focus on what *does*.

Cracking the Control Code ∿∿∿∿∿∿∿∿∿∿

Let's quiet the rooms of our souls. When I quieted my living room, I put the essentials back into the room, but only after analyzing every piece of decor. It's time to evaluate our lives with that same level of scrutiny. Here's an exercise that will help you decide whether to "do, delegate, or dismiss."

First, make a list of core boundaries. Your core boundaries are the values you want to establish for your life and the lines you refuse to cross. To get you started, consider the following ideas, and then craft value statements that work for you:

> "I don't take on work that requires me to be away from my church on Sunday."
> "Every Wednesday night and Friday night are reserved for family."
> "I will set aside the first ten minutes of every day for devotions, no matter what."

Next, make a list of everything that's on your plate right now— every task, every responsibility, every request in your e-mail in-box.

Now, use the flowchart on page 266 to help you determine what you will do, delegate, or dismiss. Be sure to keep your list of core boundaries nearby so you don't violate lines you've wisely drawn for yourself.

Use this chart regularly to help you take on God's best assignments for your life—even when deciding on the small stuff. Saying a lot of little nos can lead to bigger and better yeses. Work toward being a woman who can let go of what God has *not* asked you to do, so you can shine at what he *has*.

10

Help

The Three Best Words You Can Say to Loosen Your Control

⋀⋀⋀⋀

I THOUGHT I KNEW a lot about social media. Then three students from Stanford University gave the world something called Snapchat.

Nothing makes me feel quite so ancient as Snapchat. I break out in hives when I open the mobile-phone app, afraid that I'll accidentally send an embarrassing selfie out to the masses while standing in my underwear. The filters and features in that app confound me.

For the uninitiated, Snapchat allows friends to send photos and videos—called Snaps—to one another. But unlike a photo sent through text, photos sent through Snapchat "self-destruct" after they are viewed. The whole thing makes zero sense to me, but because I have teenage daughters whom I like to keep a close eye on, I found myself learning the ways of Snapchat. Plus, communicating in fun ways is one of my favorite things about raising teenagers. (My other favorite thing is that I no longer have to eat at Chuck E. Cheese's.)

Not long ago, our older daughter, Lydia, went away to a teenage spiritual retreat. Mobile phones weren't allowed during the weekend, a wise move that would hopefully keep students' eyes fixed on Jesus instead of screens. Lydia was perfectly fine with the rule. Until she remembered Snapchat. She was more than a little distressed that while she was away, she'd break her Snapchat streaks with a few of her besties. (A streak happens when you exchange Snaps with someone else for consecutive days. If you miss a day, the streak is broken, and the world as we know it ends in an apocalyptic fire.)

Here's something you need to know about Lydia. (Yes, she gave me permission to tell you.) She's super self-reliant, sometimes to a fault. Lydia rarely asks for help because she wants things done her way, which is to say "the right way." (Apple falleth not far from tree.)

So imagine her reaction when I volunteered to handle her Snapchat account for her, sending her friends messages and keeping those "streaks" alive with relevant content. Plus, I told her, this would give me an opportunity to familiarize myself with this handy communication app.

Cue older daughter's panic. She turned an ashen color and gave me a haunted look. But she had no choice. With resignation, she turned custody of her phone over to her mother.

I dropped her off at the retreat. When I returned home, I got down to business. It took me approximately 1.5 seconds to realize I was in over my head. I am not sure what button I pushed, but suddenly my own confused expression appeared frozen on the screen. Panicked, I found the blessed X in the corner and was able to delete the picture and recover my thin confidence. Then, I tilted my head, briefly considered making one of those duck-face expressions, but thought better of it. Instead, I sent a safe, smiling mom pic and told her friends that I would be managing things for a while. (I didn't want to try too hard to be cool but also didn't want to appear completely clueless. It's a delicate balance, people.)

I felt emboldened in my mission when one of her friends declared on Twitter the next day: "Lydia Lee's mom is keeping her Snapstreaks alive while she is away at a retreat, and it's honestly the best thing ever."

Well, *that* felt like a Snapchat win.

Thus I entered into rounds 2, 3, 4, and 5 with renewed confidence. I sent out more selfies, pictures of outdoor scenery, and—of course—a little Mama Lee love along the way.

The good news: Not one of the streaks was broken.

Now that my Snapchat mission is complete, I've had time to reflect on the lessons I learned, offered here in descending order:

4. Never take your iPhone into the bathroom with the Snapchat app open.

3. Snapchat can make rainbows spill from your mouth or dog ears sprout upon your head. (It also has a voice-changer mechanism that can make you sound like a creepy guy who offers candy to children at playgrounds.)

2. With a little practice, you're never too old to learn something new.

And, finally, the most important lesson I learned on my Snapchat Streak Rescue Mission—and the reason I told you this story today:

1. It can be so very hard to let someone help you, even when you really need it.

The Hardest Words to Say
"I need help."

Those were the absolute last words Lydia wanted to say to me. What if I broke everything? What if I embarrassed her on social media?

Like Lydia, some of us know how hard it is to ask for help. At one time or another, all people require the assistance of other people. But we often don't ask for it until we absolutely have no choice.

If that's not an accurate description of you, you are free to skip the rest of this chapter. But if the following paragraphs strike close to home, stick with me.

Self-reliant, "in-control" people are generally not good askers. "I need help" can feel like three of the hardest words to say. Example: I might actually need someone to pick up my kid from school every day for the next week, but I end up feeling like I just asked someone for a kidney.

Why don't we ask for help even when we need it? Like pretty much everything else about us, it's complicated. Here are a few reasons we avoid asking for help.

1. **We would rather be the helper than the helped.** A shift in that relationship leaves us feeling uncomfortable, and if we're honest, powerless. Oddly, the more we need help, the harder it might be to ask because the perceived power shift becomes even greater.

2. **Collaboration sounds like more trouble than it's worth.** Yes, we probably need help. But we feel like we can get it done better and faster if we do it solo. Most of us still have nightmares about leading group projects in high school and having to do most of the work ourselves anyway.

What Control Freaks Say to Make Ourselves Feel Better

- ▶ "I wouldn't be so controlling if other people would stop messing stuff up."
- ▶ "As long as everything goes exactly the way I want it to, I'm totally flexible."
- ▶ "I'm not bossy; I just know the right way to do that."
- ▶ "I'm so grateful when people offer to help. And I always give myself a few moments to pretend to prayerfully consider it."
- ▶ And in the words of Adrian Plass, "I could be a really good Christian if other people didn't mess it up all the time."

3. **We are afraid of being told no.** After finally getting up the nerve to ask, we aren't sure we could face that kind of rejection.

4. **We have never liked feeling needy, weak, or incompetent.**

5. **Asking for help is a form of surrendering control.**

If this all hits a little close to home, take a deep breath. My hand is raised, and I'm not all that excited to admit it either. I'm the woman who sprained her ankle several years ago, and when I couldn't walk to the garage, my neighbor brought me a wheelchair. I refused to sit in it. Why? That ugly five-letter word *pride*. If any of this describes you, be compassionate toward yourself. You might be relieved to know that you are, in fact, normal. People are skewed toward wanting to do it themselves. Walk through the doors of any bookstore and head straight to the self-help section for proof.

In her recent book, *The Art of Asking*, singer Amanda Palmer writes, "American culture in particular has instilled in us the bizarre notion that to ask for help amounts to an admission of failure. But some of the most powerful, successful, admired people in the world seem, to me, to have something in common: they ask constantly, creatively, compassionately, and gracefully."

She adds, "We may love the modern myth of Steve

Jobs slaving away in his parents' garage to create the first Apple computer, but the biopic doesn't tackle the potentially awkward scene in which—probably over a macrobiotic meatloaf dinner—Steve had *to ask his parents for the garage.* All we know is that his parents said yes. And now we have iPhones."[1]

I have sensed that many of my friends struggle with asking for help. Their insistence every Sunday morning that "everything is fine, just fine" is my first clue. Everything is not "just fine" all the time. Most of us need help.

On my blog recently, I tested my theory by asking, "Do you have a hard time asking for help? If so, why?" I was flooded with responses. People weren't fine after all. They needed help but were squeamish about asking for it.

Dozens of people shared their stories—people like my friend and fellow blogger Lisa Appelo. In 2011, her husband died of a heart attack at age forty-seven. Lisa and her husband had seven children, ages four to nineteen, when he passed away. Clearly she needed help. But she didn't know how to ask. A friend suggested that she keep a running list of what others could do to help, but she was unsure where to start. "I felt most things were too small, and they'd think, *They should be able to manage that,* because I did have teen boys at the time. Or they would look at this list and think, *She's asking a lot of us.*"

Asking for help requires a stripped-down vulnerability. When we ask for help, we are moving closer to an intimacy with people that feels a little dangerous. The people who come to our aid suddenly see a side of us that few get to see—the tear-streamed face, the Doritos-sprinkled kitchen floor, the hospital gown open in the back, our inability to accomplish even small tasks under stress.

It's awkward enough to ask a stranger for a quarter to fill a parking meter. How can I ask someone to help me with my kids when it seems like every other mom has no problem keeping up with the spelling lists and healthy snacks? How can I ask someone to help on a work project when it was my own fault that I said yes? And what kind of shame will I bring upon myself when I admit to the boss that I simply can't do it this time?

Listen. You need help. It's okay. *You actually need help.* Can you say it? Can you ask for it?

Do you have corners of your life where you don't let people in because you're afraid they'll mess it up? Are you scared to ask for help because you'll be "found out"? Does asking for assistance make you feel weak and powerless? Do you avoid asking for help until you have no choice at all?

When you ask for help—from people and from God— you are not weak. The truth is, you are now strong enough to admit that you can't face your problems on your own. Look, not a single soul on earth is ever so strong that she doesn't need someone to help. You are a wise woman, and you are smart enough to know you need some relief. You've known you've needed help for a while now, haven't you? You just need to be courageous enough to ask for it.

How Asking for Help Changed My Life

"I need help." I finally uttered those words a few weeks after our second daughter was born.

The memory is fuzzy because I was so low on sleep and my mind wasn't level. Hinges were loose, and I couldn't make sense of my world, so I can only see the blur of the memory now. I didn't know it yet, but I was depressed. I needed help, but I didn't want to ask for it. I was always someone's helper, never the helped. But my urgent need for mental fitness outweighed my great desire for self-sufficiency. Postpartum depression was sucking the life out of me. I felt dark on my insides, shadowy and empty, a frail ghost-person. And no amount of try-hard bootstrappiness could pull me out of it. My husband said I needed to call someone—a friend or a sister. He wrapped me in a tight hug and said there was no shame in asking. But whenever I picked up the phone to call, it felt heavy in my hand. How could I ask someone to help? And what did I really need?

One day, I called my sister Juliann. When she answered, I broke down in tears and uttered those three words: "I need help." I didn't give her a list or any ideas on how to fix what was broken. I just said those three words and bawled into the phone. She dropped everything and drove six hours north. I cried again when she walked through the door. I called her my angel for days. I couldn't get over the fact that she had left her own kids. A feeling of indebtedness weighed heavy on my insides. How would I repay her?

While Juliann was here, she and my husband drove me to the doctor. I told the doctor the same thing I told my sister: "I need help." He gave me a prescription for an antidepressant.

I still had one more place to go. Still unsettled in my spirit, I went to my closet one afternoon, dropped down on my knees by the laundry hamper, and wept before God. I was pretty flimsy in my faith at that time in my life, and I wasn't terribly convinced that God paid much attention to me. But that day I prayed a prayer that changed my life: "God, if you're there, I need help."

Anne Lamott says that help "is the first great prayer."[2] I believe that with all my heart. That prayer saved me. My sister tells me that when I walked out of the bedroom that afternoon, I looked like a new woman. That was a milestone moment for me, a moment when I found the Rock at my rock bottom. And it all started because I dared to utter three scary, beautiful words: "I need help."

Looking back, I can see why I recoiled from asking for help when I needed it most. Self-disclosure triggers a fundamental fear inside of people. If we let onlookers get too close to our truest self, they will have front-row seats to our inner wreckage. Confronted with our flawed selves, will they leave us without even a moment's notice, embarrassed by who we've become? Furthermore, if we get that close to God, where we acknowledge our need of him, will we end up bitter toward him if he disappoints us? What if we can't tolerate the times when he wrecks our flawed plans and replaces them with his?

Asking for help requires a heart-unzipped intimacy with God, who saw your need in the first place. He was waiting for you to ask. He was waiting for you to scoop up all the broken pieces of your life, lift them up to his face, and say, "Here, can you help me with this?"

God's great promise over our lives is this: "It's all under control." One of the ways that God proves his promise true is by dispatching modern-day disciples. Other humans, flawed as they are, are often the means through which God will come to your aid.

I don't know where you're at today, friend. Do you need help? I suspect you do. Maybe you're scared to ask. Maybe you're worried the words will make you look weak. Maybe you don't want to be somebody's burden.

Dare to say the words: "I need help."

These are the words that have saved marriages, sent addicts to treatment, ushered teens through the counselor's doorway, and been the catalyst for a trillion prayers of all sizes. Those three words save lives and bring people to Jesus every day. Shoot, maybe your struggle is standard-issue busyness and you need someone to do your laundry this week. Ask for it.

You are not a burden. You are a person.

When you say "I need help," you're not uttering feeble words. They may be the strongest, bravest words you ever say. You simply can't do it all. You would never expect others to do what you require of yourself. When I sprained my ankle, you would have been there in a heartbeat with a wheelchair. Let others do the same for you.

When it comes to asking for help, we can learn a lot from author Lynn Morrissey, whose inner Darling shunned help. Not anymore. "When I didn't ask for help years ago, it was because of a bad case of perfectionism, thinking if it were to be done right, I'd have to do it myself," Lynn told me. "But the truth is, my job was too big to do single-handedly." When she tried to "do it all," she performed poorly in areas where she needed others' expertise. "Now I love asking for help," Lynn said, "realizing all too well my own weaknesses and also loving to watch others operate in their own giftings."

The lesson from Lynn: When you ask someone to help, you might be setting someone up to shine.

I know what you're thinking because I've been there, and yes, all of the following statements hold true: When people help you, they might not do it the way you wanted to. They might not do it as well as you would have. They might see your scrawny backside through that gap in your hospital gown. You might have to contend with that uncomfortable feeling of indebtedness. Your "helpers" might mess things up a bit, meaning your group project gets a B minus instead of an A—but you'll still get the degree, so try to let this one slide, okay? And if some sweet mama takes your kids off your hands for a day, she might let your kids do something crazy that breaks all of the rules, like giving them ice cream for breakfast.

Friend: This too shall pass. Until then, ask for help.

Let Randy and Holli tell you how it works.

Randy, a former news editor of mine, went head-to-head

with cancer a few years ago. "I hated asking for help. I needed help with a few things, like occasional rides forty miles to daily radiation. The biggest lesson I learned from having cancer is that people truly want to be helpful. And having opened the door, people did way more than I asked."

My friend Holli, also a cancer survivor, told me this: "I had many people say, 'Gee, you don't have to do something so drastic as get cancer to ask me for a favor.'" As a single woman, Holli said, she had prided herself on being able to do a lot without having a partner. "But I've come to realize that it's a lot less isolating to ask people over who want to help you. In the end, I learned that asking for help was not revealing a weakness; rather, it was an opportunity to become closer to a loved one."

Asking for help also gives someone else an opportunity to do what they really want to do—which is, coincidentally, something you want to do as well: change the world with love. Helping people is more than a nice thing to do. It's a scriptural mandate. "Carry each other's burdens, and in this way you will fulfill the law of Christ" (Galatians 6:2). You don't want to be accused of keeping other people from fulfilling the law of Christ, do you? I didn't think so.

Remember my friend Lisa Appelo? She and her family slowly learned to ask for help—and to receive it. A few months after her husband died, her oldest son called home from college. Friends offered to buy his college books for the semester; he didn't know what to say. Lisa told her son, "Ben, they want to [help] because they love you. . . . I want you to think about this: you're headed to medical school. You'll be at a place one day where you'll be the one giving medical care on a mission trip or maybe in your own practice. You need to understand . . . what it feels like to receive so that you can give well."[3]

When Helpers Bring You to the Feet of Jesus

One of my favorite stories in the Gospels is the one about a paralyzed man who needed the healing of Jesus, but there was no way he could get to the Healer on his own. Fortunately, the man had a few good friends. Those friends each picked up a corner of the man's bed and carried him to the house where Jesus was teaching. When they got there, they discovered that the massive crowds blocked entry to the house. So here's what those friends did. They carried the man to the roof and cut a hole in it, right over Jesus' head.

Let us pause for a moment here and thank God for seeing fit to give us innovative friends who will stop at nothing to get us the help we need—whether that be a venti iced caramel macchiato from Starbucks or the adrenaline required to lift a minivan off your leg. If I were that man on the bed, I would have definitely wanted Jesus to heal me. But I would have been too bossy to get that help on anyone else's terms but my own. I would have totally bossed my friends around, telling them in no uncertain terms that they would *not* cut a hole through someone's property. They would negotiate a way through the crowd and carry me through the front door like civilized people.

But as author and Harvard professor Laurel Thatcher Ulrich famously wrote, "Well-behaved women seldom make history." My friends are not well-behaved women. They are rebellious enough to carry me where I would never go on my own. The truth about friends like that is this: They don't always do what you want, but quite often, they do what is right. They might cut a hole in the roof so they can lower you to the feet of Jesus. That's what the paralyzed man's friends did. It was an interruption that didn't irritate Jesus one bit. It impressed him. "When Jesus saw their faith, he said, 'Friend, your sins are forgiven'" (Luke 5:20). And then Jesus healed the man, who picked up his bed and walked home.

Let's go back to the beginning of the story for a moment. Everybody knew this man needed healing. But he couldn't get there unless his friends did some literal heavy lifting. He probably spoke words such as these to his friends: "I need help. Carry me to Jesus."

You never know what crazy things your friends will do when you ask them for help. But if you give them a chance, they might not only help you fix whatever's broken in your life; they might bring you straight to the feet of Jesus—in the most innovative way possible.

To follow Christ has always meant helping and serving others. But it's also humbling ourselves enough to allow others to be Christ to us, which happens in that moment when we allow ourselves to be helped.

The Vulnerability of the Ask

It takes a special kind of bravery to ask others to help us.

Over the last three years, I've seen how that kind of bravery works. My parents, two of the most kindhearted people you could meet, have faced a series of health struggles. In the middle of a recent battle, they came to our house to recuperate for about a week in December.

Both of them were in wheelchairs. Dad was recovering from surgery on his amputated leg. At the same time, Mom was in so much pain with a sore back that she couldn't walk. In the midst of it all, Anna got sick with strep throat. We joked that our house was like a hospital wing.

Our days were full of appointments, medicine deliveries, prayers, back rubs, hand-holding, inside jokes, Christmas carols around the piano, and tummy-busting laughter at unexpected moments. Occasionally, one of the able-bodied among us would fetch a glass of water, another cup of coffee, or a book we were talking about the night before. We spent a lot of time around the dinner table, watching snow fall outside the kitchen window. All of my ministry work was temporarily suspended. I wouldn't have wanted it any other way and will never regret the opportunity to serve my parents, two people who have devoted their lives to serving others.

As hours turned into days, Dad asked me to help him with a chore that he was unable to do for himself. I'm sure it was hard for him to ask, but he couldn't do this one on his own, and Mom was in no condition to help either.

"Jennifer," he said, "I hate to ask you to do this, but . . . will you wash my hair?"

"Dad," I said, "I'd be honored."

We pushed his wheelchair to the bathroom sink, and he rose on his one good leg to steady himself while he lowered his head into the bowl.

"Is the temperature good, Dad?" I asked, scooping water onto the back of his neck.

"A bit warmer would be fine," he said.

His hair wet, he sat back in the wheelchair. I poured TRESemmé shampoo from a travel-size bottle into my palms and then began to work up a lather in his hair. In the mirror, I could see him watching me.

I had an idea.

"How about you wear it like this, Dad?" I pulled his black hair into little shampoo horns all over his head, just like he used to do with my hair when I was a little girl in the bathtub. And then, after the horns, I gave a seventy-nine-year-old man a punk-rock hairdo, with his hair pulled to the middle until it stood straight up like black knives.

Our roles had been momentarily reversed, me caring for Dad this go-around. Looking at himself in the mirror, Dad laughed. It was loud and high-pitched, the version of laughter that feels like a declaration of some rare freedom. It was the perfect moment, the perfect kind of laughter. His eyes sparkled the way a boy's do on Christmas morning when he finds out that the red bike under the tree is his. This was Dad, fully alive. I could see in that moment how Dad had reached a point that I'm still aiming for: laying down one's self-protective shield and simply being fully alive.

I rinsed his hair again, and we went back to the kitchen table for more coffee and conversation. As I pushed his wheelchair up to the table, I thought about how strong Dad has been all the years I've known him—decisive in business, responsible for major corporate decisions and overseas volunteer work, a man with a terrific jump shot and the strength to carry me, piggyback style, all the way around the yard.

But I never knew how strong he was, how truly strong he was, until the day he asked me for help.

Cracking the Control Code ∧∧∧∧∧∧∧∧∧∧∧∧∧∧

All of us need help, but it's hard to look someone in the eye and ask for it. This week, let's give asking for help a practice run. The first activity is for those of you who need help but don't want to burden someone else. The second activity is for those of you who need help but are afraid to give over control to someone who might not do it as well as you.

For those of you who need help but don't want to burden someone else:

On a sheet of paper, create two columns and label them "Burdens" and "Carriers." (Or download the Burdens and Carriers worksheet on my website, www.ItsAllUnderControlBook.com/Resources.)

Under the Burdens column, write down everything—major and minor—that is weighing you down: child care, work assignments, grocery shopping, shoveling the driveway, feeding a pet, getting a ride, making a big decision.

Under the Carriers column, write down the names of anyone you think could help shoulder one of your burdens. Include the names of people who have ever offered to help you, even if it's been ages since they offered. Include the names of people with whom you could swap help. Don't forget people, such as housekeepers, whom you might be able to hire to perform some tasks to help you find temporary relief.

Then, this week, pick one burden and contact one carrier to see if he or she can help. After examining your finances, also explore whether you can hire someone to help you with, for instance, a few household chores. (That's exactly what I did while writing this book.)

For those of you who need help but are afraid to give over control:

Pick one task this week that you know is simply too much for you to handle on your own. Be willing to accept assistance from others as a trial run. As you do this, imagine yourself as a woman on her bed, like the man in the Luke 5 story. You are unable to get where you need to go without friends who will carry you. Now, in your journal or on a sheet of paper, write a prayer asking God to help you be open to collaboration. Embrace the fact that your friends, like the man's friends in Luke 5, may use different, more creative means to accomplish the tasks that need to be done. Ask God to help you welcome different means to similar ends. Ask him to help you understand that "good enough is good enough," even if it doesn't meet your standards.

11

Wait

Learning to Pause When You Want to Push

∧∧∧∧

WHEN LIFE STARTS feeling out of control and frantic, I've learned it's wise to check the level of my workload. But lately, before I check how much I am working, I check how well I am *waiting*.

I am not naturally good at waiting. I tend to be impulsive and want what I want *now*—the desired results; problems solved; everyone just getting along, for heaven's sake. I like to get my hands in the cake batter so that the desired results are achieved and everyone is happy forever and ever, amen.

This is what one might call "running ahead of God."

These days, I am learning that I need to wait on the Lord.

When I want to push, God asks me to pause. I hear his caution, way under my ribs: *Don't push. Pause.*

There are a thousand little triggers that will set off the inner impulse to push rather than pause. It's as if there's a red button attached to my insides, and when tension rises, my inner control freak presses the button: "Alert! The world needs you."

The achiever side of me wishes those moments came with my very own superhero cape and a phone booth where I could change. Then I could fling my leotard-clad self everywhere that my capable hands are needed! Just the other day, two of my dearest friends found themselves in a disagreement, and the peacemaker in me wanted to get in the middle to broker a resolution. But I felt the strong prompting of the Lord: *Don't push. Just pause.*

What I'm learning is this: The world doesn't need me to rescue it; sometimes, it needs me to step away, find my chill, and wait while God does the work he is fully capable of doing.

One reason I don't wait well is because of my helper instincts. But I avoid waiting for another reason. There's pain in the waiting. Sometimes in life's bewildering moments, we have no choice but to be still. I don't like the pain of the wilderness, of the unknown. I've wanted to push through hard times in my life—grief, disappointments, loneliness—but in those times, I'm finding God wants me to sit in the tension of waiting. I'm not to hurry, to help, or to hustle my hurts along. I am only to sit here. Sitting still in a wilderness makes me twitchy. Waiting makes me feel powerless and sometimes hopeless. But God is teaching me something very important about waiting with my unmet longings: While we're waiting, God is working.

The Waiting Room

This is the waiting room. Welcome. You know this place, don't you? When we are in the waiting room, we eventually have to make this choice: We can either distance ourselves from God or we can trust him in the wait.

This truth became so evident to me over the last three years, a season when I've logged many hours in waiting rooms—literal ones. Waiting for a friend when she had a cancerous lump removed. Waiting for our daughter Anna when she underwent procedures for a digestive problem. Waiting for Dad when he had a pacemaker put in, and then more waiting when he had part of his right leg amputated.

I've found that waiting rooms everywhere are a lot alike. An interior decorator has done what he or she could to make the place inviting. Chairs are upholstered in trendy colors. Fake greenery has been arranged in matchy-matchy ceramic pots. Magazines are fanned out on pale-colored end tables.

And now the one you love is on an operating table. Your inner "fixer" is paralyzed. Unless you happen to have a degree in neurosurgery or anesthesiology, you are clearly not needed. You are, instead, stuck—feeling rather powerless—in the waiting room. If you're lucky, a digital board identifies your loved one by a number and provides periodic status reports.

You wait for 715803 to move from "in operating room" to "surgery in progress." You wait for updates from a nurse who promised to fill you in—but never as soon as you prefer. You watch the board for news that 715803 is "in recovery room."

You wait.

My family of origin tends to be the obnoxiously loud ones in the waiting room. Humor has always been a coping mechanism for us. I suppose there could be worse things than laughing through hard times.

Last year, a couple of weeks before Christmas, my sisters, brother, and mom had returned to the waiting room because Dad was back on the operating table for the third time in a year. It has been an intensely trying season for our family, and one that we will come out of soon, Lord willing. That day in December, our family sat in a circle and laughed ungracefully as we retold stories of Christmases past. We recalled the year when our little brother, John, and I gave Dad an old fine-tooth comb for Christmas. (It was actually his comb already; we had found it under the bathroom sink, hoped he'd forgotten it was his, then wrapped it in the comics section of the newspaper. He pretended like it was what he wanted all along.) And the way we all knew that the Santa who showed up at the community center with paper sacks of candy and peanuts wasn't really Santa, or even some high-level elf. (He was the town's funeral director.) And the year we got in major trouble from Mom and Dad for laughing through the entire Christmas Eve service. (Forgive us, Lord Jesus, for all the times we've been inappropriate at church.)

Our stories in the waiting room kept us sane. Every so often, one of us would step out of our circle, somber faced, to check the digital board. A sister would whisper, "Still in surgery." We'd pause, and then we'd all start in again. Here in the waiting room, it was about stories, connection, laughter. It was about family.

There was no pushing, only pausing.

Oddly, these moments, when I sat miles away from the answers I wanted, were an unexpected gift because they caused me to consider the practice of being still. I did not flit or fly. I was a bird on a wire, wings tucked in, waiting for hope to appear, inching up from the horizon.

Waiting has compelled me to understand that I'm not in charge of the world and that my notions of control are all an illusion anyway. Waiting can feel like a weakness, especially in a culture that places a high value on self-sufficiency and "making things happen." Waiting is the opposite of sufficiency, and it leaves me exposed and armorless.

I step into so much of my life wearing armor: The armor of ambition. The armor of good performances. The armor of masks. The armor of control. The armor of trying harder. This kind of armor doesn't actually protect me like I think it will, of course. And, in fact, it can be heavy and ill-fitting. When I've worn that kind of armor, I've been like David before battling Goliath. David got outfitted in Saul's armor but realized he couldn't even move with it on (see 1 Samuel 17:39). So David went out armorless, carrying only five smooth stones. In the end, a stone was all he needed.

There is no armoring up when you're waiting, no matter how big your Goliath is. You simply wait, stripped down, vulnerable before your giant. You can fix nothing. You are not in charge now—not that you ever were—but the armor you wear on a typical day gave you a false sense of security. You finally realize there shall be no pulling yourself up by your bootstraps. This can be a very beautiful thing. When you pause—instead of push—you do all the things that matter most: You pray. You read Scripture. You sit quietly—or laugh loudly, if that's more your style—with friends and family. You practice allowing yourself to be still.

In the quietness of a hospital waiting room, the truth about God's armor is amplified (see Ephesians 6:11). In moments when our waiting-room laughter subsided, I would turn inward and whisper to my Savior, "How would we get through this without you, Jesus?" Letting down your faux armor causes you to more carefully inspect your life and discover how incredible it is to belong to Jesus: *Where, oh where, would we be without Jesus?*

Where are you today, friend? Where, oh where, are you?

Perhaps you are in a waiting room of some kind too. Perhaps you wish to act instead of wait. You want to take matters into your own hands but haven't a clue how—or even if you should. God's delay feels like a denial, and you are left discouraged.

So many people I love are waiting. One friend is waiting for God to show her what's ahead now that her sons are all in grade school. Another friend sent her last child to college and feels the loneliness of her empty nest. Another friend is consistently one paycheck away from losing her rental house, each month passing as she remains in a suspended state of waiting. My dad has been waiting three years to walk again.

What are you waiting for? The answer to your financial distress? A baby to come? A resolution to a relational conflict? The phone to ring? The wound to heal? The last twenty pounds to drop? That moment when it's *your* chance to finally celebrate?

You ask good questions for which there are no immediate answers: *Why is this opportunity slipping through my fingers? How am I going to go on now that he's gone?*

Maybe today you actually *are* reading these words in a hospital waiting room while someone you love is in the operating room, and your prayers seem to dissolve into antiseptic air as you cry out silently: *Are you here, God?*

Though he may be silent, God has not abandoned you. He is working while you wait. Do not confuse this divine delay with a definitive denial.

The work that God does in the waiting room often proves more important than the end result. Here he will give you clarity for what he wants you to do when the wait is over. Here he will draw near to you. Here you will get in touch with your essential self, the one who wasn't made to wear all that armor.

This is the greatest gift of the waiting room. Lean in close, for when you least expect it, you will sense the presence of Jesus in ways you never could have before. All of the noise that keeps you moving and running and spinning—it is gone. In the wait, hear it. Hear the hush. It's the kind of hush you hear after a great storm moves east, dragging all the whipping, thundering sounds with it.

This, I think, is what it sounds like when Jesus draws near.

A Twelve-Year Wait

In my recent season of waiting, I have thought often of a woman who spent more than a decade waiting for a miracle.

Scripture Verses to Help You Pause When You Want to Push

▶ Wait for the LORD; be strong and take heart and wait for the LORD.

PSALM 27:14

▶ Lead me in your truth and teach me, for you are the God of my salvation; for you I wait all the day long.

PSALM 25:5, ESV

▶ Therefore judge nothing before the appointed time; wait until the Lord comes. He will bring to light what is hidden in darkness and will expose the motives of the heart.

1 CORINTHIANS 4:5

▶ Our soul waits for the LORD; he is our help and our shield.

PSALM 33:20, ESV

▶ But as for me, I will watch expectantly for the LORD; I will wait for the God of my salvation. My God will hear me.

MICAH 7:7, NASB

▶ I am the LORD, and when it is time, I will make these things happen quickly.

ISAIAH 60:22, NCV

▶ You don't understand now what I am doing, but someday you will.

JOHN 13:7, NLT

▶ *Add yours here.*

You've met her in the Gospels of Matthew, Mark, and Luke: the woman who was subject to bleeding for twelve years. Perhaps her hemorrhaging was caused by a malignant disease or uterine disorder; we don't know for sure. But we do know that she sought medical care repeatedly. I imagine the hope building as she went from one physician to another, seeking a cure, only to have her hopes dashed again and again.

Scripture doesn't tell us what her treatments were, but the 1885 book *Palestine in the Time of Christ* describes the likely prescriptions she was given. They seem outlandish by today's standards. According to the author, the woman's physicians were actually rabbis. At first, they likely instructed her to drink a mixture of gum of Alexandria, alum, and garden saffron that had been pounded together and mixed with wine. If that didn't work, the rabbis would take Persian onions, boil them in wine, and give them to her to drink, saying, "Be free from thy sickness." If that didn't work, they would "take her to a place where two roads meet, put in her hands a cup of wine, and let someone suddenly coming up behind, startle her, saying to her: 'Be free from thy sickness.'" The prescribed remedies included a long succession of other archaic acts, including digging pits, burning vine branches, and more.[1]

The bleeding woman spent money on these remedies, holding out hope that something would take. No cure came. "She had spent everything she had and was not helped at all. On the contrary, she became worse" (Mark 5:26, HCSB).

Consider how physically tired she would have been after twelve years of continued bleeding. Consider the ways she would have been ostracized on account of her illness. Her waiting room must have felt like a prison. According to Old Testament law, the woman would have been considered ceremonially unclean and would have been separated from the outside world.

She waited in a private wilderness.

The details are different, but I am guessing some of you can relate to her long season of waiting—waiting for the treatment to finally work, waiting for the forgiveness that hasn't yet come, waiting for the tables to turn. Waiting can be discouraging, even devastating, when God's divine delay feels like a definitive denial.

It would have been understandable if the bleeding woman lost faith in her long season of waiting. She didn't. She lost her health and her money. But she didn't lose her faith. After more than four thousand days of suffering, she heard news about a man from Nazareth who had healed many people with many diseases (see Mark 1:34). His name was Jesus. She drew courage from her faith: "If I can just touch His robes, I'll be made well!" (Mark 5:28, HCSB).

Imagine the bravery it took to step out the door that day, into throngs of people she was forbidden to touch. Imagine how many arms she brushed against as she pressed through the crowds. Consider the gumption it took to reach out a hand and touch a tassel on the robe of Christ.

"Immediately her bleeding stopped and she felt in her body that she was freed from her suffering" (Mark 5:29).

In an instant, Jesus healed her on account of her faith.

And it happened in the most beautiful and tender way. Power left Jesus' body and entered hers. She immediately sensed that she had been cured. Jesus looked around the crowd and asked, "Who touched me?" "Then the woman, knowing what had happened to her, came with fear and trembling, fell down before Him, and told Him the whole truth" (Mark 5:33, HCSB).

Consider what the "whole truth" encompassed: her bleeding, her isolation, her fear, her risk, her belief that Jesus could heal her. Perhaps she told him that she had no money and little strength. But as it turned out, she had the most important thing of all: faith. How do we know that her faith was the key? Because Jesus said so.

"Daughter," Jesus told her, "your faith has made you well" (verse 34, HCSB).

Hear the tender way Jesus addressed her: "Daughter." It's the only time in all of Scripture where Jesus addressed someone as daughter. He spoke to her using a term of endearment. Imagine how relieved she felt to be a part of Jesus' family. In an instant, her wait was over. Jesus traded her delay for deliverance.

While she was waiting, God was working. God knew that this was the moment she was made for. This was the moment that would be an example for all who witnessed her healing miracle.

We don't always know why we are called to wait. For the bleeding woman, the waiting was an important part of her testimony.

Why might God be calling you to a season of waiting?

A part of your testimony: Perhaps like the bleeding woman, your waiting will become a part of your witness to a world in need of hope. In his divine timing, God may have you in a waiting room until the day when others can witness his power in your life.

A path to his protection: God may be calling you to wait because of the harm that would come if what you desired now was delivered. His delay may have greater purposes than your desire. I look back on my own life and think about how often I've wanted my own way, only to discover years later how disastrous the results would have been if I'd gotten what I wanted. God sees in whole what we see only in part. So that his plan can be fulfilled, there will be times when he speaks to us: *Don't push. Pause.*

A piece of his glory: Your wait may be timed so that God's glory can shine forth in ways that couldn't happen otherwise. When you are obedient in the wait, God will be faithful in the work. And you will be awed in the wonder. His delay may be setting the stage for a divine display. Jesus knows that most of us prefer immediate answers. Maybe that's why he said this: "You don't understand now what I am doing, but someday you will" (John 13:7, NLT).

Some of us may have to wait all the way to heaven to know why we had to endure difficult seasons. I can assure you of this: If you are in a season of waiting, God is not punishing you. Sometimes waiting is the result of living in a

When you are obedient
in the wait, God will be
faithful in the work.
And you will be awed
in the wonder.

broken and fallen world, where we are unable to control the hemorrhaging that comes with life on earth.

In those painful moments of unexplained delays, remember the promise of heaven. Remember how people waited for thousands of years for the Messiah to come the first time. Recall the promise that he is coming again. There will be a day with no more tears, no more death, no more waiting. As Ruth Chou Simons recently wrote: "We're not asked to grit our teeth and simply endure the heartaches of this world; we get to see through the lens of hope, and choose to bear the likeness of Christ while walking these roads between the now (all that we already have in Christ) and not yet (all that He is yet to do)."[2]

While we are in the waiting room, God is in the operating room. Like a surgeon unseen behind double doors, he is doing the work required to fulfill a perfect plan that he alone can see.

But there's more. *God is also with you in the waiting room.* He has not left you alone among the fanned-out magazines, staring at a digital board. He is with you, right now.

Often it can feel like God has gone silent during your most trying moments of waiting—those moments when you're at the end of your rope, at the end of yourself, at the end of all hope. The enemy wants you to believe you're alone in that place. The enemy wants you to believe that God has moved on to something else and that you must take matters into your own hands.

Do not confuse divine delays with a divine disappearance.

I promise you, he is right here with you. Whether your wait is twelve minutes, twelve hours, twelve days, or twelve years, he is with you.

Right here, in your heartache.

Right here, in your uncertainty.

Right here, in your chaos.

Right here, in your disappointment.

Waiting is not an in-between place. This is where real work is done in us if we slow down enough to allow it. We have already learned that surrender is not passive, but it is an active form of trust. Waiting is the same. Even in the stillness, waiting is not passive, but very active, requiring us to stay alert to what God is doing in and around us. In the waiting place, God gives us the wisdom we need for what he wants us to do when the wait is over.

Like the bleeding woman, there will come a time when you will have to do an even braver thing than wait. You will have to open a door, take a step out into the unknown, and fight your way toward the robe of Jesus Christ. This will take great faith, but that faith will have been hard-earned, built in those wilderness moments of waiting.

In faith, you will reach Jesus. In faith, you will touch the hem of his robe. And when you fall at his feet, he will turn to you and say, "Daughter, your faith has made you well."

Cracking the Control Code

Ask God to help you discern when you need to pause instead of push.

Are you a Driver? If so, you are likely tempted to say yes at every turn. Pause instead of push. For instance, allow yourself at least twelve hours of prayer and consideration before making new commitments. Then *choose best over busy*.

Are you a Devoter? If so, you are likely to want to "help" those you love. Pause instead of push. For instance, instead of intervening to resolve conflicts in your children's lives, avoid taking matters into your own hands if the outcome doesn't depend on you. If you have older children, consider asking them questions to help them find their own way rather than constantly offering a steady stream of advice, or worse, doing the work for them. Instead of *doing* it for them, help them *develop* good habits. *Choose develop over do.*

Are you a Darling? If so, you are likely to put in long hours to meet unrealistic standards of perfection in your work and in yourself. Pause instead of push. Decide in advance what a reasonable amount of effort is and then stick to it. Instead of assuming that it's not perfect, determine that some things are good enough. *Choose good enough over perfect.*

In times of distress, your inner control freak may want to bust out of the waiting room and try to fix everything. Pause instead of push. Ask God to build your faith and help you wait. This season could lead to a part of your testimony, a path toward his protection, or a piece of his revealed glory.

In what areas of your life is God calling you to pause instead of push?

12

Whole

Relaxing Your Body . . . Your Mind . . . Your Soul

∧∧∧∧

I AM IN CANCÚN. I flew from Iowa to this place of endless summer, where I'll spend a long weekend with girlfriends whom I rarely see. I almost didn't come, and I had my reasons, including the familiar "I am too busy." I was behind on the deadlines I'd set for this book, and I don't do well with missed benchmarks.

Back at home, God had been giving me the contents for this book, but only in bits and pieces. This book has been constructed the way one puts together a puzzle—but without having the advantage of seeing the picture on the top of the box. You can imagine how my inner control freak has dealt with this. I have to laugh when I recognize the truth that writing a book on control has felt utterly out of control. (There's a lesson from God in this, I am sure of it.)

So yes, I've been behind. But I couldn't deny the longing for a change of scenery, even if it set me back further. I felt God nudging me, *Go. It's all under control. This book will be waiting for you when you return.*

Now let me clarify something. I don't need to run off to Cancún to "find myself." But it definitely seemed right to go. This was the invitation set before me by friends, many of them also Christian authors who understand the ups and downs of ministry. I needed some time with in-the-trenches girlfriends, so I said yes to Cancún.

That's where you find me now, sitting on a balcony on the seventh floor with my laptop, as the sun rises over the Gulf of Mexico. The palms are waving their morning welcome, while the ocean turns an impossible vivid blue.

Yes, I am writing on vacation. Yes, I brought my computer. And in the first hours of each day, I come to the balcony to write. Surely, by now, this does not surprise you. I understand that this may feel like a contradiction; I've come to Cancún to rest, after all. But sometimes moving to a new environment offers the freedom to find new words.[1] If I find words here, I don't want to forget them because those might be the words we both need; and it seems like too much responsibility to write all of my thoughts on scraps of napkins and room-service menus and then be expected to safely transport them home.

I've certainly made time to rest as well as work on this

vacation. Yesterday I had a massage inside one of the resort's grass-roofed huts. I was lying facedown, with my head pressed into one of those circular pillows that has an open space in the middle so you can breathe. Above me, the blades of a bamboo fan turned slowly, generating a small breeze. I felt my body relax itself, as if it instinctively knew how to do this. Small candles in glass votive holders flickered in the corners of the room.

My massage therapist shuffled quietly around me, arranging tiny bottles of essential oils and checking the temperature of hot stones, which would be used in my therapeutic massage. Eyes still open, I could see her slippered feet move toward me.

She whispered a handful of words that ushered me into a state that can only be described as pure tranquility: "Relax your body . . . your mind . . . and your soul."

It was such a small thing, this tiny collection of words spoken in a soothing Latina accent. She probably delivers those same eight words to every woman stretched out on her table. But as she spoke, something welled up inside of me. As I breathed in the scent of eucalyptus, I thought I might cry. Her words, though hushed, released a dynamic energy that surged from my heart to my fingertips. "Relax your body . . . your mind . . . and your soul." Her words reminded me that I am a *whole* body, mind, and soul. I am interconnected, and I am also connected to God.

I am a *whole person*.

Obviously, right? Except I don't act like a whole, connected person. I act like a dissected person, operating one part at a time, trying to run the show and keep all the parts moving. My survival instincts kick in, and I block off my emotions. I become a human robot in yoga pants, trying to make it through the day without losing control of my emotions and everything else.

In the massage room, I had a sudden awareness of my whole self, and a stunning realization of how my regular life had often gotten severed and sliced. I do not operate as a seamless "body-mind-soul," despite the fact that God designed me that way. I treat myself as a fragmented person: body, then mind, then soul, and back around again. I run my *body* ragged. Later, I work my *mind* as hard as it will go. I tend to my *soul* when I can. I treat the three parts of myself as separate entities. I arbitrarily divide my life between the secular and sacred.

When I operate like this, I am in survival mode, like a soldier on a battlefield, resolutely doing what needs to be done. And it seems like it's working. And then, when I'm off the battlefield, when I'm finally safe at home, that's when I finally let loose and have a good cry. I never understood why that happened—why I would cry only when I finally felt safe. Why didn't I cry on the battlefield? But then my friend Bonnie Gray, a Christian author who has battled post-traumatic stress disorder, told me why. A soldier doesn't tend to experience trauma when his bravery is required on the battlefield. A soldier experiences panic attacks after he gets home. That's when he is safe to face what was too difficult to process before.[2]

That moment on a massage table was my safe place. There was no battlefield. I was at home with myself. And in that moment, someone else acknowledged me as a whole being—body, mind, and soul, interwoven. I can't begin to tell you how "seen" I felt by God through the words of a stranger whose only job was to give me a decent massage. It was like God was standing nearby, so present to me. It reminded me of the very first question that God asks in all of Scripture: "Where are you?"[3] God already knows the answer. It seems God asks the question not so much to get a response, but mostly to let us know he's near. We aren't alone after all. He sees us.

I felt so seen in that moment; I felt so whole.

I suppose the therapist's words struck so deeply because I had already begun to see a shift in how I was living my life. I had begun to view life through the lens of God's sovereignty. Months ago, I had taken God off of my to-do list (chapter 7) and had begun to hand God my to-do list so that he might order my days. Furthermore, every morning before I began my work, I had been praying: "God, help me to make choices today that honor your plans for my life." This was a tangible way of acknowledging that God calls the shots.

The wholeness of God—his omniscience and omnipresence—had become discernible. Under the spinning blades of the bamboo fan, I felt another kind of wholeness—not only of God, but also *of me*.

This is what I felt in my core: I am a person of body and mind and soul. I am not a pixel or a machine. My body is not meant to be run ragged, all gears on high all the time. My mind is not a separate entity, nor does it compute on its own. My soul is not excised from the rest of me, a wisp of a thing that waits for heaven and will float away when I die. My soul is more than some inner ghost that I encounter in spaces where I meet Jesus during my quiet time.

My soul—the Greek word *psychē*—means "the vital breath, breath of life, . . . the seat of affections and will." In the Greek, *psychē* means "a human person." Listen to this: Psychē is "the direct aftermath of God breathing (blowing) his gift of life into a *person*, making them an *ensouled being*."[4]

I am this: Whole. A person. An ensouled being. The direct aftermath of God's own breath.

This is my essential self.

The Great Exhale of God

It is the same for you. You are a whole person. You are the direct aftermath of God breathing life into you. Breathe that truth in. *Inhale the great exhale of God.*

What would it look like today if you quieted everything inside of you for a few moments? Step off the battlefield. Set down the load in your arms. Feel all your feelings, and be at home with who you are. Turn to face your self—your whole self—to be hushed by the one who breathed you into being. You are a remarkable being of body, mind, and soul— a human person, a psychē.

Pause right now to ask yourself these questions:

Where do I still feel dissected, pulled in too many different directions?
When am I operating as if I am only a body and a mind, with a finite and fragmented existence?
In what ways does this make me feel soulless and empty?

I am a little terrified to admit this, but I can get so fragmented, pushing my mind and body so terribly hard, that hours can pass without me even giving Jesus so much as a thought. In these moments, I am full steam ahead on my agenda. When I take a sober assessment of my life, I can see where my control tendencies get triggered, ushering me into the danger zone. This happens when my inner Driver traps my soul behind a series of urgent obligations. I feel tired, even after a regular night's sleep. I can tell I'm irritating people with my short answers and lack of eye contact. These are all warning signs. Are you beginning to see

A Few Places Where I Have Felt the Exhale of God

- In a warm bath, with a favorite book and vanilla-scented bubbles
- On a Lund fishing boat, with my dad
- In the delivery room, after the pain subsided, when I saw each of my children for the first time
- In the backyard, catching fireflies in jars
- Around a dinner table, with good friends and take-out pizza
- Atop the Cliffs of Moher, suddenly aware of how small we truly are
- At the altar, with my bread half-dipped in the cup
- On a balcony, writing this one for you
- *Add yours here:*

yours? Can you sense where your obligations pull you away from your essential self, your psychē?

In fragmented times, it's impossible to accept the rest that Christ offers. This is Christ's invitation to us: "Come to me, all you who are weary and burdened, and I will give you rest. Take my yoke upon you and learn from me, for I am gentle and humble in heart, and you will find rest for your souls" (Matthew 11:28-29).

In that verse, the word for *soul* is, again, *psychē*. Jesus promises rest for our psychē, our whole being. If we live disjointedly, ignoring our psychē, we will never be able to live in wholeness on our busy days. Instead, we will function as fragmented beings while trying to carry out God-assigned tasks. The answer here is not to quit our regular lives, take more naps, or simply "stop being busy." In a perfect world, we would all come to Cancún together once a month, but this isn't that world. We've got to figure out how to live as whole people, even as we function in our everyday busy lives. When Jesus invites us into this kind of wholeness, he doesn't say, "Take a vacation, and you will find rest for your souls." He doesn't say, "Stop working, and you will find rest for your souls."

This is what Jesus instructs us to do: Set down our yokes, then take up *his* yoke to function under *his* authority, in service to him and in imitation of him.

I love Eugene Peterson's rendition of that verse on rest in *The Message* paraphrase: "I'll show you how to take a real

rest. Walk with me and *work with me*—watch how I do it"
(Matthew 11:29, emphasis added).

How did Jesus do it? How did he maintain a restful spirit
as a whole being, even as he worked?

It's safe to say that Jesus worked harder than anyone, in the
history of ever. His responsibility while on earth was great,
culminating with his work on the cross. He healed, forgave,
fed thousands, debated scholars, and preached to enormous
crowds. His time here was short—his earthly ministry lasted
only about three years—but he accomplished more than our
minds can fathom. John tells us we don't even know half
of what Jesus did in that time: "Jesus also did many other
things. If they were all written down, I suppose the whole
world could not contain the books that would be written"
(John 21:25, NLT).

Yet Scripture reveals that he never did his work in a fragmented, dissected way. He engaged his whole being—body,
mind, and soul—often lifting his hands and face to heaven in
prayer immediately before carrying out the work God called
him to do. He engaged his whole self—his psychē.

Jesus modeled a restful spirit while working, and he also
modeled the full stop. He spent a lot of time alone with the
Father. He spent many hours praying. He retreated to private
places. If Jesus needed full-stop rest, we do too. There are
times when we need to completely cease all busyness. (More
on that in the next chapter.)

But true rest isn't about your lack of activity; it's about the
state of your soul. Rest is the ability to access your psychē,

even as you work with your body and mind. Even as you fold the seventh basket of laundry. Even as you text your friends, fill out the report, or nurse the baby at 3 a.m.

Relax your body . . . your mind . . . your soul.

What does this mean for us?

First, remember this: God gave you a body. Your body was created to take you to amazing places. At times, you may find that your body is stronger than you ever imagined it could be. Your body can do courageous things: run marathons, hold bedside vigils, grow babies, and brave the Black Friday crowds at Best Buy and come out with your salvation still intact. You are not a wimp. God may call upon you to carry out Kingdom tasks that leave your body physically weary at times. But if you don't engage the psyche with the body, you are living a dissected life. You will be unable to access the "rest for your soul" that Jesus promises in the midst of your work.

In the same way, your mind was designed by God to think creatively in the work he has called you to do. He gave you wisdom, a wicked-funny sense of humor, the ability to solve conundrums (like fourth-grade math) and broker peace treaties among squabbling siblings, all while crushing it at the office. There will be times when your mind will be required to push harder than you thought it could and understand more than you thought possible. You are no dummy, sister. But if you don't engage the psyche with that brilliant mind of yours, you are living a dissected life.

I'll say it again: True rest isn't about your lack of activity; it's about the state of your soul. True rest isn't a place you go;

it's a Person you know. True rest is the unshakable presence of God, breathing his gift of life into your whole being—body, mind, and soul—whether you are at your busiest or absolutely still in his embrace.

On that massage table, I realized this: Surrendered living is much more than "doing less." It's being more of who God created you to be. It's living as a whole person, moving as a whole person, breathing as a whole person. It's inhaling the great exhale of God and turning around to love God with your whole self. Jesus calls you and me to that kind of living. "Love the Lord your God with all your heart and with all your soul [psychē] and with all your mind and with all your strength" (Mark 12:30).

We are called to love God *with our everything.*

We can love him with our passions, our talents, our energy, our mobile devices, our calendars, our emotions, the hardest work of our lives, the most fulfilling moments of rest, our gifts, our hands, our money, our actions, our reactions, our dinner parties, our yard work, our doctor's visits, our moments in the waiting room, and our times when we're facedown beneath the bamboo fan.

Come to me, Jesus said, and I will give rest to your souls.

Touch the Sky

Here I am again on the balcony. I did what I promised you I would do. I took a break. I embraced the wholeness of me, my psychē.

I found it early this morning when I wrote words for you.

As always, I imagined you sitting beside me. I can't begin to tell you how much this invigorated me. So in my work, I embraced the wholeness of me. I encountered that wholeness again this afternoon with a plate full of guacamole under a big umbrella, while watching the waves roll in and marveling that God commands the ocean to only go so far. And then at 3 p.m., I took a ride in the sky. It was Jessica's idea. She wanted to parasail. It was a three-seater, so Lisa and I said yes to Jessica's invitation.

Jessica was a little nervous about the whole thing, and since I had gone parasailing once before, I pretended to be braver than I actually was. What she didn't know was this: In my head, I was prewriting the news stories that would announce our tragic deaths.

We walked down a long dock, stepped into a powerboat, sped into deeper water, and were harnessed into a parasailing apparatus.

"Are you scared?" Jessica asked me as a man snapped us in.

"Um, a little. Yeah." I laughed, gripping so tightly to the canvas straps that my knuckles shone white through my skin. I had a strange feeling in the pit of my stomach, the way you feel when you're crazy and brave and afraid all at once. And then . . . *up*!

Up, up, up we flew into the sky, with a smiley-faced parasail above us. The rope stretched, taking us 250 feet high above that water, blue on blue. Far below us, a sea turtle meandered near the surface. As we rose higher, that weird feeling of doom dissipated. Tranquility returned. Here was all of me, whole—vulnerable, clumsy, awakened, a bit out of control, and wildly free. Body. Mind. Soul. All here.

I drew air deep into my lungs and let it out again. It felt like a warm fog coasting in and out of me. I was inhaling the exhale of God.

I felt my fists loosen, how they fell away from the straps. And then I opened my hands and lifted them, higher and higher toward the cloudless dome above me, higher still, like I could touch the sky.

Cracking the Control Code ∧∧∧∧∧∧∧∧∧∧∧∧

Are you feeling fragmented? Consider what you might do to live what Ann Voskamp calls a "one-piece life." Ann has compared life to a seamless one-piece garment. Such a garment was a rare possession for a Jew in biblical times. Ann says that kind of garment is a great metaphor for life. All that we do is interwoven into one—our relationships, our dreams, our work, our passions, our parenting, our creativity. Nothing is fragmented or torn into categories. Nothing is arbitrarily divided. She writes, "We wear God's seamless silk when we mindfully offer everything we do as a sacrifice to God."[5]

Paul explained it like this: "So here's what I want you to do, God helping you: Take your everyday, ordinary life—your sleeping, eating, going-to-work, and walking-around life—and place it before God as an offering" (Romans 12:1, MSG).

Imagine now your life as a garment. Identify the frays, the torn seams, the pieces that have become detached from God. In times of disconnectedness, perhaps you are like me. Perhaps your mind strays from him—even for hours—and thus you stray from your essential self, to the point where your shadow side emerges. You find yourself feeling overly responsible and needing to call all the shots. Consider finding new ways to remember that God is in control of your life and wants to partner with you.

- On busy days, set an hourly alarm on your phone to remind you to take a five-minute walk with Jesus. Let him speak into your psychē.
- Try placing a chair (or picturing one) in whatever room you're in. Invite Jesus into the chair. Imagine him sitting with you

wherever you are, not as a watchdog for your behavior, but as a friend and work partner engaged in the work with you.[6]

- At the end of every day, take an honest assessment of your day. Did your work get in the way of who you want to be as a person with a psychē? What triggered your shadow side to emerge? If this kind of question stumps you, ask someone you trust to tell you what they saw in you that day.

- Make a list of activities that activate your awareness of your whole self: body, mind, and spirit. Maybe it's a massage, a brisk walk with the dog, or an especially invigorating hour of work when you tap into your whole self. This could be an activity that brought you joy in the past but that you've let slide. Now commit to doing one of those activities by the end of the week. As you do it, inhale the great exhale of God!

13

Rest

The Real Reason You Feel Busy but Not Productive

∧∧∧∧∧

BY EIGHT THIS MORNING, my iPhone was dinging with messages.

One daughter forgot to have me sign a permission slip, so *would I please come to school right away to sign it?* An editor e-mailed to ask if I would consider writing an article for her magazine. A friend started a meal sign-up for a new mom and wondered if I could help out . . . tonight. All of the requests held a sort of urgency. Of course, I would do what I could, but I could feel my internal fuel gauge creeping toward *E* before the day had really begun.

Full stop. I needed to connect with God.

I didn't want to start my day by handing God my agenda instead of asking him for *his*. I want my work assignments to flow from my soul alignments. So I opened my Bible to the Gospel of Mark and began reading. Right then, my phone vibrated in the next room, set into a frenzy by repeated messages in a group text. It vibrated so furiously that I thought it might knock itself right off the table.

I laughed out loud at the irony and the timing. Because in that moment, I was reading the story where Simon tells Jesus: "Everyone is looking for you!"

You know the feeling, don't you? Everyone is looking for you too.

In the Bible story, Jesus had spent the previous evening healing sick and demon-possessed people outside Simon's house. "The whole town gathered at the door."[1] The next morning, Jesus got up very early and went off to pray, alone. Jesus wanted to connect with God, so he left the village. But his solitude didn't last long. Simon, who didn't know where Jesus had gone, apparently needed him *right that instant.*

You can practically hear the exasperation in Simon's voice when he finally found his teacher: "Everyone is looking for you!"[2]

A typical day in the life of Jesus: Never an end to the work, only an end to the day. His workdays were crammed with a range of assignments, some planned and some spontaneous. He tended to the sick, comforted the afflicted, afflicted the comfortable, and preached to the heartbroken—and then awoke to more of the same. While Jesus may have been tempted to sleep in many mornings, he would rise very early, walk to a deserted place, and spend time with the Father. More than once, his time of refreshment was interrupted. If Jesus had an iPhone, it would have been pinging with requests from everyone who stood waiting at Simon's door.

Don't you feel a kinship with Jesus in this? If you feel like "everyone is looking for you" and you can hardly steal five minutes with the Father, Jesus totally understands. Some days, it feels like everyone wants you to be the solution to their lost library book, the stain on the shirt, the empty spray can of squeeze cheese. Everyone wants you to sign up for the meal drop-off or the leaf-raking party. The reason they're looking for you is because they know they can count on you. The Devoter in you loves ferociously, and you don't want to disappoint anybody. You keep helping and loving harder still. Some days that means that the last person you take care of . . . *is yourself.*

You and I have probably both come to realize that we're always going to have a lot on our plates. We are high-velocity women who love connecting with people, taking on new challenges, and helping where we can. *Dear Jesus, let us serve you until the day we die!*

If you're like me, you regularly put service first and rest second. Rest has often looked like hitting the wall, tank on empty, with nothing left except the satisfaction of a job well done. I don't think that's what God intended.

While writing this book, I realized that I needed to do something different. I wasn't designed to rest *last*. I was designed to rest *first*, so that my work would flow out of rest. Any other approach is the equivalent of leaving the gas station with a clean windshield, a bag of sriracha almonds—and only a quarter tank of gas.

I don't want to get so busy that I can't hear Jesus' voice. I don't want to get so wrapped up in everyone else's agenda for me that I forget to consult God about his. Meeting with God for daily replenishment reminds me of these basic truths:

- I am not everybody's solution.
- I don't have to be in control of everything or in charge of all the outcomes.
- I don't have to put myself in the center of everything, nor must I allow myself to be dragged there.

The demands on your life will keep coming, and God will ask you to do hard things. But I promise you this: *God will never ask you to stretch yourself so thin that you don't have time for him.*

With so many demands on you, how will you know which way to turn? Jesus shows us how, again and again. Like Jesus, begin with rest so you'll know what's best.

The busiest man to walk the earth found time for replenishment. Every day, Jesus was pulled in a lot of different directions, but before deciding which way to go, he intentionally dwelled in the presence of God. Surely Jesus' time with the Father helped him prioritize. His work assignments flowed from his soul alignments. Rest first; work second.

Who knows how much time Jesus had before Simon and

his companions rushed in that morning. Scripture reveals that it was enough. Because after that soul alignment with the Father, Jesus knew his daily work assignment. Jesus made it clear that he wasn't being called to follow the agenda that Simon or anyone else in town had for him. He would go where the Father led him.

Jesus said, "Let us go somewhere else—to the nearby villages—so I can preach there also. That is why I have come."[3]

If Jesus needed to meet with God, then how much more do we need to do the same? We are not going to magically know which direction to go, nor will God wave a wand to bring rest to our souls. He is asking for our cooperation here. Our work assignments will flow from our soul alignments.

But first:

Listen. Breathe. Go to a quiet place.

Rest.

A Work-Obsessed, Rest-Deprived Culture

Confession: Resting has always been hard for me. There's always something to be written, folded, wiped, cleaned, answered, washed, driven, pushed, finished, fed.

Did you watch the *Downton Abbey* series? If so, you may remember Violet Crawley, the dowager countess of a great English estate at the turn of the twentieth century. In the show, this grand old lady famously asked the question: "What is a weekend?" Whether it was Wednesday or Saturday, the work was done by servants. The food was prepared by in-house cooks. The Dowager Countess of Grantham had seemingly unlimited time for leisure, rest, letter writing, horse races, and gatherings in the drawing room with guests.

Fast-forward to today, and consider the weight that same question holds in our work-obsessed, rest-deprived culture. "What is a weekend?"

I've trekked through long seasons of busyness in which my work bled into my weekends. Sundays were as hectic as Mondays. I needed to dress the kids for church, arrive in the sanctuary early to put the finishing touches on a PowerPoint for the pastor, deliver snacks to the kitchen, teach junior-high Sunday school, make dinner at home afterward, help the girls with homework, answer a few e-mails that I'd neglected, and make organizational lists for the coming week.

Indeed, *what is a weekend?*

We live in a society where we are more accessible and busier than ever with our hands-free Bluetooth headsets, constant availability, multitasking phone apps, and more. Even places where we used to simply exist quietly with our own thoughts—like the waiting room of a dentist's office or in line at Target—we can now use as an opportunity to check Facebook or answer a brief e-mail.

I asked a group of women at church the other day, "What do you do to truly rest?" Over and over, they told me: "I feel like I'm too busy to rest." We have more means than ever to get on top of everything, but we're finding instead that everything is getting on top of *us*. All these gadgets that were supposed to make us sane end up leaving us swamped. Social availability has become our souls' adversary.

Research indicates that the drive toward busyness is especially prevalent in women. Women often feel "guilt if they aren't as busy as other people, or guilt if they take any time off for themselves."[4]

I've carried that kind of guilt. I've looked around and seen moms homeschooling five kids while running a nonprofit. I've wondered, *How does everyone else do this?* So I minimized my need for rest, thinking I had no right to fuss when I compared my life to someone else's.

Motivated by guilt, I overscheduled myself, thinking, *If she can do it, I should too.*

Listen to Your Engine

Let's stop should-ing ourselves and start replenishing ourselves. We need to listen to our bodies instead of pushing them. What if, when we heard our bodies begging, *Go into lower gear*, we actually paid attention?

As an example, let me introduce you to my first car. It was a red Volkswagen Beetle with a clutch and stick shift. It always reeked of fuel, which meant that I smelled like a gas station. My Slug Bug died an untimely death in 1989 when it started on fire on an Iowa highway. I rescued my French horn from the backseat and walked down the deserted highway, crying under a half-moon sky, waiting for someone to let me hitch a ride.

The car had been my first major purchase, bought with my

lifeguarding paychecks. I didn't know how to drive a stick shift at first but learned by listening to the sounds it made. In its own way, the car had a "voice." When the car was in too low of a gear, it made a high revving sound. That was my cue to shift to a higher gear. As I continued to accelerate, the car's voice would prompt me to shift into even higher gears. Lower gears were reserved for slower drives through the center of town.

In the same way, busy people need to listen to the voice within us. Sometimes life calls for acceleration, speed, and efficiency. But one of the best gifts we can give ourselves is to stay in lower gear from time to time. When we hear that high revving sound in our lives, we will be tempted to shift to higher gears. And sometimes life will require us to do just that. But sometimes that high revving sound is a warning to slow down, stay in lower gear, and maybe enjoy the scenery.

I am learning to listen to the voice within. I am learning to live in lower gear when my internal engine starts revving. This is a grace I offer myself, to intentionally connect with God—in lower gear—before I accelerate again. This is the only *me* that I get. I don't have to run myself into the ground. I don't have to maintain a go-bananas pace. I don't have to say yes just because I am generally capable of running at high capacity.

Neither do you. Sometimes the bravest thing you can do is listen to your body's engine when it says, "I need rest."

Too Busy Not to Rest

You might be thinking, *I'm too busy for lower gear. I'm too busy to rest. Everybody needs me.* Do you remember the classic book on prayer, *Too Busy Not to Pray?* The same principle applies to rest.

We are too busy *not* to rest.

The busier you are, the more you need to rest.[5] In order to successfully complete all the tasks on your list, you may actually need more quiet time than a person who isn't as busy as you.

It's not always the work that torments you. It's your lack of rest *from* it. You don't need to quit everything; you need a break so you can refuel. According to an article in the *Harvard Business Review*, "Taking time for silence restores the nervous system, helps sustain energy, and conditions our minds to be more adaptive and responsive."[6]

Here's what will suffer if you don't take time to recharge: that work you care so much about. (All of the achievers are now sitting straight up in our chairs.) It's true: A lack of adequate rest can hinder your creativity and ability to tackle your workload. Research shows that the biggest obstacle to creativity is being too busy.[7] When you're resting, you are granting your precious mind the elasticity to daydream, wander, and wonder. That may actually lead to breakthrough ideas in your work.

Our modern, gadgeted life impedes that kind of creativity. We can trick ourselves into thinking we're resting by bingeing on Netflix or scrolling through social media. We might not realize that our minds are still operating at high gear with activities that disguise themselves as rest. Emma Seppälä, science director of Stanford University's Center for Compassion and Altruism Research and Education, writes: "If our minds are constantly processing information, we never get a chance to let our thoughts roam and our imagination drift."[8]

In other words, we can't dream if we won't rest.

The world is filled with ambient noise, and it can be hard to hear God's voice above it all. Maybe it would be easier if God were a screamer, but he's more like a whisperer, with his still small voice.[9] If I have a lot of noise around me—even in the form of the silent iPhone scroll—I can't hear God.

Lindsay Sterchi, mom of twin toddlers, learned the hard way what happens when she doesn't get the rest she needs. She told me, "Without rest, I'm not very fun to be around—just ask my kids and husband. I get irritable way too quickly. I lose perspective on the bigger picture of life, and the little things seem bigger than they really are. I get in this fog where I'm going through the motions of life but not really living intentionally."

The answer for her: finding rest in small pockets of time each day. "Rest means that when the kids nap, or after they've gone to bed, I'm not going to zone out on TV or scroll through social media, which might *seem* restful but ends up being draining." Instead, she does something that feels life-giving—without feeling guilty. Her escapes: reading a book, journaling, or simply being still, alone with God and her thoughts. Maybe your escape *is* Netflix, and if that's the case, *you do you*. But make sure it gives you life instead of draining your energy.

In the past few years, I've learned how to quiet the *outer* noise. My biggest challenge is silencing the *inner* chatter.

I know the value of resting in Jesus, but it's like my brain won't stop moving in fifteen different directions. Corralling my thoughts is like herding a nursery full of fork-toting toddlers who just learned how to walk and are weeble-wobbling their way toward electrical outlets on opposite sides of the room.

Take, for instance, one of the places where I go to escape the noise: my bathtub. I'll toss a bath bomb in the water and sink into the warmth. There's no TV. No iPhone. Yet even here, my mind is running on high gear. I often receive some of my best writing inspiration in the bathtub, which is why my friend Cheri gave me a set of child's bathtub crayons. (Yes, part of this book was written on the walls of my tub.) So while it might *look* like I am resting, I'm actually still working.

God is reminding me that my brain needs rest as much as my body does. I loosen my mind by simply dwelling with him: "Abide in me, and I in you."[10]

Resting in God serves two purposes: First, rest allows you to intentionally connect with God. God wants to meet with you, not simply to give you the day's marching orders. He wants to be with you because he likes you. Second, rest calms the noise around you so you can hear God's clear direction. In the same way Jesus knew to "go somewhere else" instead of returning to Simon's house, you can hear where God actually wants you to go when everyone comes looking for you.

Perfect Gifts for the Overachiever in Your Life

- Bouquet of freshly sharpened pencils

- Hand-lettered motivational poster

- Lint roller

- Multicolored stacks of sticky notes

- Anything from The Container Store

- Daily planner with color-coordinated tabs

- A screen-printed T-shirt that says, "I'm silently correcting your grammar"

- This book (I have not yet mastered the art of subtlety.)

Resting in the midst of an exciting journey can feel counterintuitive. But if we don't, we will suffer. Our work will suffer. We will get stretched too thin and will be ill-equipped to give our best.

In the quiet, God might reveal a surprise.

That's how it happened for me a few years ago. I quit my part-time job teaching journalism at a nearby college. I loved the classroom. I loved telling students how journalists are the first eyewitnesses to history and the first people to share it with the world. How we go into press conferences one day and small-town diners the next day because that's where the news is made. I loved telling students how we are paid to be the hot breath on the neck of a good story.

And how one-sentence paragraphs rock.

(Even when those paragraphs are sentence fragments.)

I loved telling students how we are called by God, as Christian journalists, to be curious, to ask good questions, and to fight for the just-right word. I felt utter delight when a student—ruddy-cheeked with optimism—pressed her latest news story, faceup, onto my desk: like she knew she had dug deep enough to find a universal truth. I loved those rare moments when a student's story made me cry—for all the right reasons, praise Jesus.

But I had to leave what I loved because I had become overscheduled.

"Well, what will you do now that you quit?" That's the question a friend asked me a few days after I shared my decision with her. We were sitting at my kitchen table, and she leaned in with wide eyes, wrapping her hands around a warm mug.

"I . . ." My own eyes darted. "Well, I will . . . uh . . ." I stammered, trying to find words to come up with a list of important new projects that I would tackle. I realized in that moment how I had seen quitting as a spiritual weakness.

As it turns out, quitting might be the thing you and I do that makes us strongest. If done with intentionality, quitting might lead us to true rest—so we can be our best at a few things instead of mediocre at a lot of things.

I finally told my friend the truth: "What will I do? Well, I'm going to breathe. That's what."

Prune Away, Jesus

That year, I felt like I was under the shears of a pruner, who cuts away the good to make room for the better.

Jesus says that God cuts off worthless branches that don't bear fruit, and that type of pruning makes sense. "He cuts off every branch of mine that doesn't produce fruit."[11] Cool. I'm down with that. Prune away, Jesus.

But Jesus does more than cut off unproductive branches. He also cuts good ones—perfectly healthy, fruit-bearing branches. "He prunes the branches that do bear fruit so they will produce even more."[12] That pruning hurts. Why cut away a perfectly good branch? Because, Jesus says, that's how you'll produce even more.

The pruning season of my professional life led me into a quiet space where I could hear God's direction. That pruning season eventually led me to you—through my blog, my books, and a speaking ministry.

For years, I was a news reporter, producing good fruit. That branch was pruned. Then I taught others how to be news reporters, producing good fruit. That branch was pruned. You can prune the girl from the newsroom, but you can't prune the news out of the girl. Because these days, I'm writing about the best news story of all: the Good News of Jesus Christ.

Maybe someday God will prune books and blogs from my life. Until then, I will lift my chin high and step forward into my calling. Yet I cannot afford to forget this truth: The more responsibility I take on, the more I actually need rest. If I say yes to something new, something else has to give. What is that "something"? It can no longer be my rest. It can no longer be my family.

God has pruned many healthy branches from my life, and they've fallen at my feet. It's heartbreaking to see good fruit in a pile on the ground. But in those moments, standing amidst the branches, I can open my hands to his best for my life.

I can only sense his best when I rest.

Sometimes our best will look like a mad sprint, a sweaty slide across the finish line, out of breath. Sometimes it will look like a slow walk.

Either way, let's go with Jesus.

It Is Enough

This morning, I took my daily rest outside, on gravel roads carving narrow alleyways between the corn and soybean fields. The crops were huddled together, swaying, a gentle motion, and it felt like a tide slowly rolling out. God graciously arranged for me to walk through parted green seas. Sometimes, on cool mornings like these, I put music in my ears, and I run until my lungs burn and my breath comes out in short, hot bursts. But this morning, I decided to walk a single mile. Just one. My feet treaded a slow pace, a pace that felt like the equivalent of rest—the kind of rest that lets me daydream. I thought about you. I thought about this book. In those slow minutes, with an orange sun sliding up the eastern sky, God helped me unravel a knot in this chapter, and it was a relief.

Because of my rest, I could give you my best.

But something else happened, out under that wide sky shot through with the color of flame. When I was walking, I saw what I'd never noticed before—even though I'd run along this road countless times. I noticed wild roses clustered on the banks of ditches. There were elegant patches of clover. And because I didn't have my headphones, I heard what

I hadn't heard before—wind rustling the grasses, the sigh of trees, birds opening their beaks for loud trills in faraway branches, . . . and my own steady breathing.

Maybe I go through life too often running from one moment to the next. Next book chapter. Next life chapter. Next item on the to-do list. Next project. Next run. Next duty. I'm often pushing, hustling, moving—wanting to do better than before, to get it "all under control," gain mastery of my torrent of thoughts, and prove to myself that I can jump over the next hurdle—all the while hoping I can make a difference in this big world of ours.

But sometimes when I pause long enough to listen to my body, I realize it just wants to walk. It doesn't want to reach a new milestone. It doesn't need to be useful. It just wants to take the next step. And that's enough. The wild roses are enough. The patches of clover are enough. One foot forward? Enough. My own steady breathing? Enough.

This is what I stand to risk if I don't slow down: Running will become frighteningly routine. I will forget what it means to walk. I will miss the green seas, the morning yawn of trees, the quiet whisper of Jesus, saying, "I've got this."

So here's to taking one mile at a time at our own pace—a sprint, a jog, a walk . . . a crawl. Just take the next step.

It is enough.

Cracking the Control Code 〰〰〰〰〰〰〰〰〰〰

1. Take an inventory of your life, noting the internal and external signs that you lack adequate rest. Circle the ones that resonate most with you.

   Forgetfulness
   Tearful outbursts
   Irritability
   Curtness with people you love
   Resentment toward the work you used to enjoy
   Isolation from people
   Lack of concentration
   A sense of "drowning"
   Fatigue, even after a regular night's sleep
   Indecisiveness
   No time for other things you love, like friends and long dinners

   If you circled three or more of these, you are likely under a rest-deprived stress that can send any of us—Drivers, Devoters, and Darlings—over the edge into our shadow selves. (See page 255 for a reminder of what happens when we are triggered by stressors.)

2. Think about the core boundaries you set in chapter 9. How have you let your increasing load of obligations bleed over your boundaries? Commit to staying firm on your boundaries and reclaiming lost territory. Review your "Do, Delegate, or Dismiss" list so you can make room for rest.

3. Here are a few ideas to incorporate more rest into your life.

   Instead of scrolling, go strolling. Everybody has time for rest. How can I be so sure? Because that's the time we use to check social media. Put down your iPhone for the fifteen minutes you would've spent on Instagram and take a walk instead.

   Don't let your "yes" encroach on your rest. If you say yes to something new, evaluate everything else on your list to see what might have to go. Refuse to put rest on the altar of sacrifice.

   Let your work assignments flow from soul realignments. If "everybody is looking for us," our souls and agendas need realignment so we can hear clear directions from God.

   Protect the freed-up time you have already created. God prunes all of us, but achievers try to immediately fill those pruned spaces. Protect the space that God created for you. Downtime is okay; in fact, it will make you more productive in the work you were designed to do.

14

Guarantee

Plans, Pinings, and a Promise

∧∧∧∧

It was raining outside today, and I sat under the porch awning on the front step of my house, overlooking our soon-to-be-harvested cornfields. Sitting here, I thought of you. I thought of us.

I am overwhelmed with gratitude to Jesus for letting me take this journey with you. I'm so glad you said yes to this invitation. In the beginning, Jesus told us the same thing he's been saying all along: "Help is here." He has proven himself faithful to his promise.

Jesus has done a mighty work in my heart. I thought I was going to be writing this book for *you*. Turns out, God was asking me to write it for myself as well. When I was about halfway through the manuscript, I thought, *Wow. I've been in the middle of a sacred experiment with God, and I didn't even realize it.* Over and over, God asked me to trust him and walk deeper into relationship with him. I didn't realize how far away I'd strayed from trusting God with my whole life. When I asked you to "crack the control code," God was busy cracking the code in my life.

Friend, I was a tough nut to crack.

Sometimes, the cracking was painful. Yet I can't deny what I gained in return. I reclaimed lost intimacy with Jesus. I finally got over that icky feeling that if I spent time with God, I was going to miss out on something else. I can honestly tell you this: I didn't miss a thing—not the important things anyway. This is the rock-bottom truth: You will never regret time spent with Jesus. And you will never regret a decision to trust God.

During my own journey, I learned that I wasn't a woman to be "fixed"; instead, I was a woman whom God wanted to redirect. God never once told me to be a different person, to stop achieving, or to tear up all of my to-do lists. Instead he channeled me in a more fruitful direction. Now I can finally let go of what God has *not* asked me to do, so I can shine at what he *has*. I am, at last, arriving at my essential self.

I hope you've felt that freedom too. You don't have to be more than you are. But you also don't have to be less. *You do you*, my friend, *you do you*. You have permission to apply the right amount of elbow grease and then stand back to watch what the Lord does.

Remember this: You surrender outcomes, but you don't surrender effort. God will call you to do hard things, and with his Spirit pulsing through you, you are more than able.

As I sat on my front step this morning, I wished you could have sat there with me. We'd share LaCroix and cheddar popcorn, and we'd talk about what Jesus has been up to. Let's imagine, for a moment, that you are here.

This is what I'd want to talk about:

1. plans
2. pinings
3. promises

So on the last leg of this journey, I invite you to my front step. Let's talk.

Our Plans

Back when I was a news reporter, I wrote a four-day series of articles on the state of rural America. It was the best news reporting and writing I ever did, requiring months of research and interviews. I poured my whole self into that work and received a national writing award for the series, called "Tattered Countryside." The framed award made me feel proud, not in a braggy, "I got their approval" way, but in a way that reminded me of the value of hard work and purpose.

I capped the series with a personal essay that said, in no uncertain terms, that rural life held nothing for me. I had my

You surrender outcomes, but
you don't surrender effort.
God will call you to do hard
things, and with his Spirit
pulsing through you, you are
more than able.

own plans—and they would unfold in a city, end of story. I wrote that there was no logical reason I could ever make a viable life amidst the cornfields. Well, we know how *that* turned out. Check out our view from the front step for proof. Here we sit, you and I, watching rain patter softly on the fields of my family's farm.

God planted me in a place I never wanted, and that's where I found what I really *needed*. From tiny seeds, my faith grew. This is where Jesus captured my wandering heart. I shudder to think what would have happened if my take-charge self had steamrolled her way toward her own plans rather than surrendering to his.

Today, I'm wearing a baseball T-shirt screen-printed with the words "Keeping It Rural." God willing, I'll be "keeping it rural" and keeping it real for many years to come on this patch of Iowa. But I know that I don't get to decide any of that. It's all under control, but that control is not mine.

"Many are the plans in a person's heart, but it is the LORD's purpose that prevails."[1]

As you consider your plans, I offer these gentle words: Tend your seeds wherever they may fall, my friend. You never know what might be growing, even now, in unexpected places.

Let's continue to pray this prayer: "God, help me to make choices today that honor your plans for my life."

We don't have to stop making plans, but let's hold those plans loosely. We may look into the rearview mirror one day and be relieved that our well-laid plans never came to pass.

A few months ago, I found an old prayer journal that I kept for many years. I'd written down names and just enough details so that when I looked back on it, I remembered afresh what I had prayed for. I flipped through the pages to find evidence of broken marriages, severe illnesses, addictions, betrayals, prodigal sons. There were prayers for new jobs, church moves, and absurdly bold dreams.

With the gift of hindsight, I can see the hand of God. He moved some mountains just the way I asked him to, and he moved some mountains farther than I thought possible. I also saw that he didn't move every mountain. He didn't part every sea. He didn't fulfill my every desire. And some of that stings. There are still unresolved conflicts, great unknowns, and ginormous "whys" when I turn the pages in my prayer journal.

But through this journey, there are four things I'm beginning to believe about our prayers and our plans:

1. Not a single second is wasted when we take our desires before the Lord.

2. We will never regret praying bigger than we dared think was possible—the kind of prayer that a smiling God might remark about when we get to heaven: "Wow, child. You remember what you prayed for way back when? That was one ambitious prayer!"

3. We will someday thank God that he didn't always do what we wanted.

4. He won't move every mountain. He won't part every sea. But we can trust him still. One day, his plan will make total sense. "As for God, his way is perfect."[2]

Our Pinings

Sitting here on the front step with you, I also thought about our pinings. Here's what I'll bet we both have pined for, for much of our lives: guarantees.

Guarantees that we could make it through this life in one piece, unscathed by pain and suffering. Guarantees that we could offer that kind of protection for our loved ones too. Guarantees that when we fully surrendered to God, it would all turn out right. My whole life, I've wanted those kinds of guarantees. But there are no secret pills or self-help books that offer that kind of protection.

In the end, that's why I wanted to grip my life tight. I never wanted anything bad to happen, and somehow I lived under the crazy notion that if I worked hard enough, I could move closer to the guarantee.

Yes, I've pined for guarantees.

Wouldn't those guarantees be nice? Picture it: We'd come into the world and be handed a list of instructions for a guaranteed happy, pain-free life. On it, someone would have written where to find the accident-proof car, the magic pill to forgo illness, the impenetrable hand sanitizer, the least dangerous routes to everywhere, the right prayers to make everything turn out fine, the surest way to make ends meet, the right political leaders who would fix all the wrong things.

But there are no guarantees like that.

In the year that I wrote this book, our broken world has proven that point over and over again. Hurricanes, earthquakes, fires, mass shootings, a refugee crisis, terrorism, and more rocked this planet. I felt the constant urge to look over my shoulder at what was coming up behind me. And if I wasn't looking backward, I was tempted to look ahead, hoping a forecast would offer clues on how to handle strife on the horizon. Some days, I wanted to bubble-wrap my family and keep them all safe in a gated fortress, forever and ever, amen.

This life isn't safe. Most of us have faced loss, and if we haven't, we will. If you live a normal life span, the road you take will include suffering, and even your best efforts to plan for it will fail.

Yesterday I read the first few chapters of a book on suffering, written by one of my favorite modern-day theologians, Tim Keller. In it, he points out that no matter what precautions you take, what systems you put in place, how much money or power you have, you cannot avoid suffering: "Human life is fatally fragile and subject to forces beyond our power to manage. Life is tragic," Keller writes. When pain and suffering come—and they will—we learn what we suspected all along, he says: "We finally see not only that we are not in control of our lives but that we never were."[3]

Maybe those statements make you want to run to the store for that bubble wrap, after all. Resist the urge. A bubble-wrap existence isn't really living, is it? It's hiding.

We can't live like that, trying to figure out how to survive so we can show up in heaven unscathed. We can't live life as if we're going to survive it. No one ever has. We all come with an expiration date, and one day, we will see what we've been pining for all along.

Turns out, there really *is* a guarantee.

The Promise

Our guarantee is a promise from God himself. The guarantee is that we will never walk through this life alone—no matter how out of control life gets, even when we find ourselves in the dark.

> Even though I walk through the darkest valley, I will fear no evil, for you are with me.
> PSALM 23:4

The guarantee has never been that we would avoid the valley. The guarantee is that we wouldn't walk through it alone.

What God does this? What God in the history of gods actually walks with his people through pain? Our God. That's who. He did more than walk. He bled. Jesus actually plunged himself into this world to provide us a real and lasting hope. He didn't simply say some nice words about being with us. He lived it.

Take a moment to ponder the remarkable work of Jesus. Take in the potency of the final words that he spoke over us from the cross: "It is finished" (John 19:30). What a promise!

Where in your life do you need to know that it's finished? Where in your life are you still trying to earn your way, prove your worth, control your future, or get what's already yours in Christ? What responsibility do you take as your own that was never yours to begin with?

"It is finished" invites you to end all the striving.

Today, hear your victor speak those three words over you. In the Greek, the phrase "it is finished" is actually represented by a single word: *tetelestai*. That word means "finished" or "completed." Get this: *Tetelestai* also means "paid in full." The word *tetelestai* was written on receipts in New Testament times to show that a bill had been completely paid. What a great reminder that when Jesus died on the cross, he paid our debt *in full*. *It is finished.*

We don't need to pay our way.

It is finished.

We can stop trying so hard to be more, to be enough, to prove ourselves.

It is finished.

There was a tremendous debt on us, long before we took our first breath. The wrath due us was upon his shoulders. And with his last breath, Jesus uttered the words, "It is finished."

Paid in full.

That is the startling truth of the marvelous cross. When we try to add to it, we are saying to Jesus, "Thanks, but I can do this on my own. I appreciate the agony you endured, but it wasn't quite enough."

Let's linger at the cross. Let's see it for what it is: full payment for a debt we owed but simply couldn't pay. We bring nothing to the cross—but our sin. We owe nothing to Jesus—but our complete adoration. We hand him our lives. He gives us a guarantee. And he didn't stop with the promise of eternity. He equipped us to make it through this life until we see him face-to-face. Jesus gave us the fruit of his own Spirit.

Here's what God's Spirit produces in us: "love, joy, peace, patience, kindness, goodness, faithfulness, gentleness, and self-control."[4]

We've spent a whole book talking about control, and it seems fitting to talk about self-control before we reach the final pages. Self-control is the last of the fruit, but it's certainly not the least.

I used to think that self-control was simply about not indulging in our desires—as if God's main purpose here was to keep us from eating the whole bag of Funyuns. Because of my narrow view of self-control, the Darling in me always treated this virtue as one more thing I needed to control. It was all about keeping my longings in check, to make sure I was following the rules.

Turns out, self-control is so much bigger than that. Let's step back and see the whole picture. Self-control is actually *God's* control at work in us. *Strong's Concordance* defines *self-control* as something "proceeding out from *within* oneself, but not *by* oneself."[5] Which means that we don't do this in our own power. The Greek word for self-control is *enkráteia*, which means "true mastery from within." For the believer, this kind of self-control can only happen by the power of God working within us.

That means we have more control than we ever dared imagine, with more power to wield it than we ever thought possible. There's actually quite a bit you can control. Here are a few things you can start with today: your effort, your perspective, how kind you'll be, what you'll stand for, what you won't stand for, how you treat other people, how you treat yourself, how much time you give to worry, how much time you give to God, if you let them keep you down, if you stand back up again, how honest you are, your gratefulness, your attitude, your words. And so much more!

You, my friend, are not powerless. That is the promise of God at work in you. That is the guarantee.

Let this be our manifesto:

Today, I refuse to be held back, chained down, worked up, or shoved ahead. I am committed to God's agenda and God's purposes, and I ask for God's peace so I can pursue God's glory.

I abstain from useless brooding, worrisome thinking, frantic pushing, or jittery striving. I want the self-controlled mind of Christ, not the anxious mind of chaos.

I yearn to make choices every day that honor God's plans for my life rather than stubbornly sticking to my hour-by-hour plans. I hereby sentence my inner control freak to life in prison with no parole. That way, I can truly be free. I will need God's strength to do this.

So I come to my Lord weak. And in this weakness, I know that I can borrow his strength. I understand that the strength he gives was costly for him but free for me, bought at the cross. But he didn't stop with the gift of his strength. He also purchased with his blood the following: forgiveness, grace, hope, and forever love. All of the above are renewable resources, available each day to anyone in need (which is pretty much all of us).

I believe in strength for today and bright hope for tomorrow. I am confident that—based on God's unbroken promises since the beginning of time—he will provide both.

Today, I stand on those guarantees.

To the enemy, I say: Not today, Satan. And not tomorrow either. I am in the firm grip of Christ.

To Jesus, I say: I'm counting on you alone. I will keep my eyes fixed on you instead of diverting my focus

Things You Can Control

- ▶ Your effort
- ▶ Your tongue
- ▶ Your thoughts
- ▶ Your perspective
- ▶ How kind you'll be
- ▶ What you'll stand for
- ▶ What you won't stand for
- ▶ How you treat other people
- ▶ How you treat your own self
- ▶ How much time you give to worry
- ▶ How much time you give to God
- ▶ If you let them keep you down
- ▶ If you stand back up again
- ▶ How honest you are
- ▶ Where you'll focus
- ▶ Your gratefulness
- ▶ Your reactions
- ▶ Your attitude

to the following distractions: my circumstances, my problems, my agenda, or my own good works.

And no matter what my to-do list tries to tell me, I refuse to believe that I am missing out on anything when I am spending time with God.

I submit myself to Jesus—for his great purposes and for his great glory.

Signed,
Me

Make It All about Jesus

Well, we made it, didn't we? God was right all along: "It's all under control." Let's make our whole lives *all about him.*

MAKE IT ALL ABOUT JESUS

I managed my life like a white-knuckled driver.
Sweat on the brow, I pushed like a striver.
Hustled to care for my family and friends
While trying to keep up with the latest of trends.
When lo, in my heart there arose a faint sound.
Was a voice so distinct, with a truth so profound:

"Make it all about Jesus."

Still, I pushed a bit harder (for I thought that I "must").
I served, and I gave, and I guided and fussed.
Made lists. Took on more. And found that at night,

I was drooping and weary; I lost my delight.
My whole life was fueled by "Yes!" and by "Do!"
The voice came again, "Be still, for it's true:

"This is all about Jesus."

And then one day, I gave up on "should."
I gave thanks for all that was right, true, and good.
I gave up on hustle. Let strivings all cease.
I lit a small candle and felt a warm peace.
For at last I had come to know in my heart,
That God wanted more than my lists and my charts.

For it's all about Jesus.

Let me henceforth be known by my faith in a Maker
(who never assigned me to be Earth's caretaker).
I'm done with the wearying life of pretender,
My heart wants to sing a sweet song of surrender.
I open my hands, and my heart, and my soul,
And God answers, "Dear child, it's all under control."

I believe it at last, this truth that is ageless:
Life means the most when it's all about Jesus.

Jennifer

Acknowledgments

I WANT TO LET YOU in on a secret about writing Christian books. There's a 100 percent guarantee that Jesus will get up in your face about the very topic you're addressing. I wrote my first book about approval, so of course I struggled with wanting approval. I wrote my second book on happiness and then walked through an Eeyore-ish season in my life.

Well, I'm no dummy. That's why I told Jesus I wanted to write a book on the topic of beaches. This was the ultimate spiritual throwdown. I was pretty sure I had brilliantly set myself up for a challenge from God: "Go forth, therefore, and determine the quality of beach sand in Maui and compare it to the beach sand in Tahiti." Clearly, I am willing to suffer for Jesus.

But then I forgot about my beach-book idea. Instead, I was led to write this book—because I *needed* this book. Turns out, you needed it too.

When I finally got honest about my own struggle with

control, I heard you say: "I do too." To all of you who stood with me, I offer my deepest thanks. Your "I do too" turned into this book.

I thank God for you, and for these:

To Scott, my favorite farmer. Your signature phrase, "God's got it," has been hard-earned. I love you more than words can express.

To Lydia and Anna. Your dad and I dearly love you. We pray that you grow into young women who know that "it's all under control" when you live under the lordship of Christ.

To Lisa Jackson. I am deeply grateful for you. On the hardest days, your calming voice of encouragement played on repeat in my head.

To Sarah Atkinson. This is our third book together! Our continued partnership means so much to me. I hope this book finally solves all of your problems. ~ wink ~

To Kim Miller. You're a genius editor. I'm afraid I wouldn't know how to write a book without passing the baton to you.

To the entire Tyndale team, including Kara Leonino and Jillian Schlossberg (acquisitions), Eva Winters (designer), Kristen Magnesen (marketing), Danika King (copy editor), Sharon Leavitt (all-around angel—I mean, author relations), and Maggie Rowe and Kristen Schumacher (PR).

To Lisa-Jo Baker. I can't thank you enough. You know why. I feel like I owe you a kidney or something.

To Suzie Eller. I was twenty thousand words into this manuscript but found the courage to start over after I told you how I was struggling. You asked me this: "What is the offer that Christ is extending to you and your reader?" And that was the start of a new beginning.

To Cheri Gregory. Your input and encouragement made such a difference.

To the entire Hope*Writers community, and especially our Hope*Writers Circle. You were among the first to believe in the message, and you made me feel brave until the last word was written.

To my CAM sisters on Voxer: You have been a wealth of knowledge and friendship. Erin Odom, thank you for bringing us together.

To Christin Lazo and Kris Camealy. Our little prayer group has always been a safe place.

To Pastor Jo. How do I begin to thank you for the hours of consultation, prayer, and spiritual direction? You've been an answer to prayer in more ways than I can express.

To Kaitlyn Bouchillon. Your wisdom and creativity in my online ministry have been invaluable. You are a godsend.

To my launch team. Your generosity matters far more than you can imagine. I simply couldn't carry this book out into the world without you. You are truly the best cheerleaders on the Internet!

To my family and dear friends. Your unspoken names are written into the pages of this book and into my life. Thank you for putting up with me on the regular.

To you, my reader. Thank you for accepting the invitation. I'm glad we found each other on the side of a dusty road with our empty tanks and our great rescuer, Jesus Christ.

And to you, Jesus. You told me you could fix the mess I'd made, and you weren't playing. Because of you, I recovered a peace that I had forgotten was possible. Thank you for the relentless reminders that, no matter what, "it's all under control."

Control Code Continuum

Use this tool to determine whether you've moved from healthy to unhealthy patterns of behavior. Read the descriptions to determine your zone, and then consider responding as suggested.

Healthy Zone:

- Maintaining busy schedule without feeling overwhelmed
- Engaging and enjoying time with God; growing in faith
- Handling everyday stresses with relative ease
- Approaching life with self-confidence
- Feeling energized and focused
- Making time for others
- Willing to ask for help
- Getting enough sleep
- Performing well
- Having fun

Response: Keep it up! Continue to make dwelling in God a priority. Be proactive with decisions.

Caution Zone:

- Resenting those who don't pull their weight
- Difficulty shaking worrisome thought patterns
- Feeling more anxious than usual
- Not sleeping well
- Limiting social activity
- Zoning out
- Racing mind, even when resting
- Viewing time with God as a chore
- Lagging concentration

Response: Pray for God to reveal areas where you need to change your patterns or attitudes before this gets out of hand. Talk with someone you trust.

Unhealthy Zone:

- Feeling irritable
- Difficulty focusing
- Losing self-control
- Occasionally feeling worthless
- Experiencing fatigue, with sleep patterns worsening
- Foreboding sense of fear/worry
- Neglecting spiritual growth

Response: Seek spiritual guidance. Review what you need to "do, delegate, or dismiss" (see chart on page 266). Ask God to reveal where you've overstepped your limits.

Danger Zone:

- Feeling completely out of control and a sense of doom
- Experiencing an overwhelming sense of worthlessness
- Severely neglecting relationship with God
- Feeling anger, rage, panic
- Sinking into hopelessness
- Regretting words and deeds
- Offending others
- Isolating self
- Feeling exhausted and burned out

Response: Seek counseling now. Ruthlessly examine responsibilities. Have a trusted adviser show you where you need to "delegate or dismiss" (see chart on page 266) and where you should "hang on" or "let go" (see chart on page 265).

The Three Control Characters

IN CHAPTER 4, I introduced you to the Driver, the Devoter, and the Darling, the three control characters I identified while researching and writing this book. Below you'll find more detailed descriptions of each category. These types have different motivations, strengths, and shortcomings—places where assets morph into liabilities.

Most likely, you will see yourself in one or more of these summaries. You'll see what it looks like when you are at your best—and at your worst. Understanding both your assets and your triggers can help you learn to stay on top of what is yours to manage and relinquish control when it doesn't serve you or those around you.

THE DRIVER

Energized by: external order, efficiency, and goals

Tends to be: a planner, predictor, group leader

Her superpowers: If you ask her to do the work, it's as good as done. At her best, she can handle a lot of things at once. She's a decisive, goal-minded, confident, methodical, long-range planner. She remains absolutely committed to whatever God has called her to do.

Why we love a Driver: In the event of the Apocalypse, you will thank God for the Driver in your life. She's the one with stocked cellars and two years' worth of bottled water. She's also a godsend if you're away from home and need any of the following: aspirin, Band-Aids, a Tide stick, sewing kit, chewing gum, stethoscope, chocolate, umbrella, or small generator. (All of these items are in her purse.)

She is motivated by: a deep desire to keep all the parts moving, maintain order for the good of all, and give her best to her calling.

Her kryptonite: She comes undone by others who don't do their share or unexpected emergencies. Because of her tendency to say yes and believe that "because I'm capable I should," she ends up burned out and stressed.

At her worst, a Driver: is a workaholic who sets unrealistic goals. She feels as if it's all up to her and runs the show in order to prevent disaster. She doesn't delegate because she thinks she can do it better. Doesn't always "take time to smell the roses." As a result, her many responsibilities can make her anxious and bossy. She longs for a break but is scared of what will happen if she takes one. Because she is future-focused, she tends to ruminate on what *could* go wrong. She can feel like she's one step away from tragedy or devastation unless she puts the proper plan in place.

Goofy habits of a Driver: She may have to go back home because she's afraid she forgot to turn off the stove or unplug the curling iron. She may agree to lead the committee and then resent everyone else for not stepping up to do it.

MOTTOS FOR HEALTHIER LIVING:
- "Worry changes nothing. Trust changes everything."

- "The forecast calls for a 100 percent chance of needing Jesus."

KEY VERSES TO LEAN ON:
- "When I am afraid, I put my trust in you" (Psalm 56:3).

- "The LORD will fight for you; you need only to be still" (Exodus 14:14).

A DAILY PRAYER TO HELP DRIVERS:
"Dear God, never let me be so busy that I can't hear your voice."

THE DEVOTER

Energized by: genuine concern for the people she loves most

Tends to be: caring, generous, loyal, zealously doting

Her superpowers: She is a woman tuned in to others' needs. She happily gives help where it's needed, and at her best, she is self-sacrificing out of her desire to be the hands and feet of Jesus to a world in need of hope.

Why we love a Devoter: She legitimately cares about what's going on in every area of your life. She will drive you to the airport at 4 a.m., remember your cat's birthday, send care packages to other people's college kids, and bring soup when you're sick. She's the kind of mom who—*praise Jesus!*—effectively kills lice before sending the kids back to school. Should you need any of the following items, she has plenty on hand: books on "sleep training," hand-lettered "thinking of you" greeting cards, those plastic thingies that go in electrical outlets, SPF 700 sunscreen, bubble wrap to protect the kids.

She is motivated by: a deep desire to protect the people she loves from pain. She lends a hand because she fears what will happen to you if she doesn't.

Her kryptonite: when people no longer need her help or refuse her help. She becomes worn out from doing so much for others. As a result, she tends to overhelp other people while neglecting herself.

At her worst, a Devoter: believes she knows what's best for everyone she loves and gets upset if someone makes a decision without her input. Constantly the helper, rarely the helped, she may experience burnout and be overbearing. She isn't just a helicopter parent, but she is also a lawn mower parent, cutting the preferred path for her children.

Goofy habits of a Devoter: She may hover over a sleeping child to make sure she's still breathing—even though the child is a senior in high school. She may repeatedly show her husband how to load the dishwasher, because if she doesn't, how will he ever learn?

MOTTOS FOR HEALTHIER LIVING:
- "Our God, who's got the whole world in his hands, also holds the ones I love."

- "Today, I will let faith—not fear—be my first response."

KEY VERSES TO LEAN ON:
- "The battle is not yours, but God's" (2 Chronicles 20:15).

- "There is no fear in love. But perfect love drives out fear, because fear has to do with punishment. The one who fears is not made perfect in love" (1 John 4:18).

A DAILY PRAYER TO HELP DEVOTERS:
"Dear God, help me to remember that you treasure my loved ones even more than I do."

THE DARLING

Energized by: internal order; a desire to be the best version of herself

Tends to be: one who plays by the rules, attends to details, focuses on self-improvement; more likely to control herself than others, unlike Drivers and Devoters

Her superpowers: She passionately pursues goals and holds fast to high standards of personal integrity and behavior. At her best, she's dependable, loyal, well-liked, and a hardworking member of the team. Rightly aimed, her excellence and enthusiasm reflect God's power at work within her.

Why we love a Darling: She will push hard toward goals. She doesn't give up easily, inspiring others to do the same. When she's working in superpower mode, she's a great role model for your kids. She's also the friend who knows which fork to use, knows whether skinny jeans should be cuffed or not, and tends to see the best in others, readily offering praise to motivate those around her.

She is motivated by: a desire to have internal control more than external control. She is less likely to try to determine the behavior of others, but she feels the need to be strict with herself. She fears what you'll think of her if you see her flaws.

Her kryptonite: criticism. Her inability to meet all of the unrealistic expectations she sets for herself can lead to feelings of worthlessness.

At her worst, a Darling: is a perfectionist, approval seeker, and people pleaser. She fears abandonment and is afraid of being average. While she tends to be dependable, she can sometimes procrastinate or not come through because she fears failure. She feels anxious over the pressure to perform and often presents an idealized version of herself. Her own unreasonably high standards leave her feeling frustrated and burned out. She also tends to avoid situations that may require vulnerability.

Goofy habits of a Darling: She's the mom who "helps" kids create Pinterest-perfect Valentine's boxes, making the rest of us look bad. She decorates her own house so that it looks like nobody lives there. She assumes you're not being truthful when you pay her a compliment.

MOTTOS FOR HEALTHIER LIVING:
- "His banner over me doesn't say, 'Prove yourself,' or 'Try harder.' His banner over me is love."

- "When I don't have it all together, I will remember that with Jesus, I have it all."

KEY VERSES TO LEAN ON:
- "Even before he made the world, God loved us and chose us in Christ to be holy and without fault in his eyes" (Ephesians 1:4, NLT).

- "Fear of man will prove to be a snare, but whoever trusts in the LORD is kept safe" (Proverbs 29:25).

A DAILY PRAYER TO HELP DARLINGS:
"Jesus, help me live my life like I believe what you say is true."

Your Turn

Do you know which type you are?

As you considered these three descriptions, you may have had an "aha" moment. Perhaps you discovered something new about what makes you tick, how you've tried to cope with the hardships of life, or the ways you've been controlled by fear. With such information, you will be equipped to make better choices and course-correct when your inner control freak is triggered. I also hope you have a better appreciation for the marvelous contribution you make to the world around you!

If you're still not sure whether you're a Driver, a Devoter, or a Darling—or if you just want to have fun seeing if your suspicions are right—be sure to take the quiz online at www.ItsAllUnderControlBook.com/Resources.

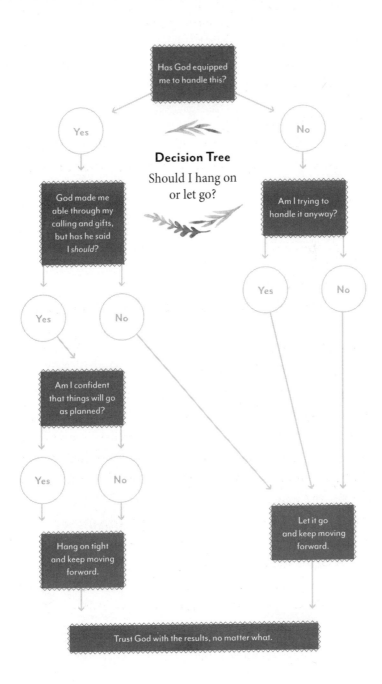

Has God equipped me to handle this?

Decision Tree

Should I hang on or let go?

Yes

No

God made me able through my calling and gifts, but has he said I *should*?

Am I trying to handle it anyway?

Yes

No

Yes

No

Am I confident that things will go as planned?

Yes

No

Let it go and keep moving forward.

Hang on tight and keep moving forward.

Trust God with the results, no matter what.

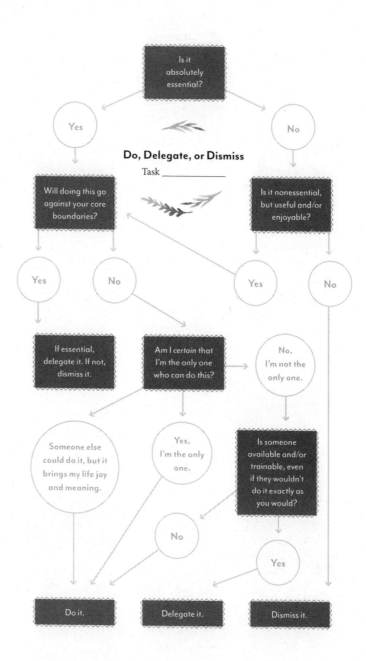

Is it absolutely essential?

Yes

No

Do, Delegate, or Dismiss
Task _____

Will doing this go against your core boundaries?

Is it nonessential, but useful and/or enjoyable?

Yes

No

Yes

No

If essential, delegate it. If not, dismiss it.

Am I *certain* that I'm the only one who can do this?

No, I'm not the only one.

Someone else could do it, but it brings my life joy and meaning.

Yes, I'm the only one.

Is someone available and/or trainable, even if they wouldn't do it exactly as you would?

No

Yes

Do it.

Delegate it.

Dismiss it.

Endnotes

CHAPTER 2: ILLUSION

1. Raymond S. Nickerson, *Cognition and Chance: The Psychology of Probabilistic Reasoning* (Mahwah, NJ: Lawrence Erlbaum Associates, 2004), 304.
2. Susie Larson, "The Connection between Fear and Control," *Live the Promise*, Faith Radio, October 15, 2016, http://myfaithradio.com/2016/resting-gods-love/.
3. Experts also refer to these hypervigilant folks as snowplow or bulldozer parents. Whatever you call them, these are the moms and dads who bring out all the heavy equipment in an effort to keep their kids safe!
4. T. M. Luhrmann, "The Anxious Americans," *New York Times*, July 18, 2015, https://www.nytimes.com/2015/07/19/opinion/sunday/the-anxious-americans.html.

CHAPTER 3: AWESOME

1. "How Being Busy Became a Badge of Honor," *MPR News*, March 21, 2016, https://www.mprnews.org/story/2016/03/21/the-drive-to-be-busy.
2. Michael Zigarelli, "The Epidemic of Busyness among Christian Leaders," CT Pastors, *Christianity Today*, July 2007, http://www.christianitytoday.com/pastors/2007/july-online-only/100405.html.
3. George H. Dawe, *We Knew Him: Personal Encounters with Jesus of Nazareth* (Bloomington, IN: WestBow Press, 2012), 39.

CHAPTER 4: SUPERPOWERS

1. Jill McCormick, "Another Achiever Goes Rogue: An Interview with Jennifer Dukes Lee," Common-Sense Grace for the Try-Hard Girl (blog), August 8, 2017, http://www.jillemccormick.com/jenniferdukeslee/.

CHAPTER 6: LET GO

1. See 1 John 4:18.
2. Matthew 28:20, MSG
3. See Mark 9:24, HCSB.

CHAPTER 7: SWITCHEROO

1. James 4:8, ESV
2. Francis Chan, *Basic: Who Is God?* Volume 2, video series (Colorado Springs, CO: David C. Cook, 2010), accessed at https://www.youtube.com/watch?v=bgQ2wiTefmQ.
3. Jennifer Dukes Lee, *Love Idol* (Carol Stream, IL: Tyndale House, 2014), 83.
4. Mike Rosmann, "Suicide Death Rate of Farmers Higher than Other Groups, CDC Reports," *Iowa Farmer Today*, August 5, 2016, http://www.agupdate.com/iowafarmertoday/opinion/columnists/farm_and_ranch/life/suicide-death-rate-of-farmers-higher-than-other-groups-cdc/article_3274056b-50a2-5e22-91d5-7da991a996ea.html.
5. See Colossians 1:17.
6. John 2:5

CHAPTER 8: CLUELESS

1. Alan Menken and Howard Ashman, "Poor Unfortunate Souls," *The Little Mermaid* soundtrack, Walt Disney Records, 1989.
2. Deuteronomy 34:4
3. Mark 3:21
4. Psalm 119:105, KJV
5. This prayer is also included in a foreword I wrote for Suzanne Eller's book *The Spirit-Led Heart* (Bloomington, MN: Bethany House, 2018) and is printed here with permission. I highly recommend this resource for anyone seeking to move from a self-led heart to a Spirit-led heart.

CHAPTER 9: ROOM

1. Be sure to check out Myquillyn's book *Cozy Minimalist Home* (Grand Rapids, MI: Zondervan, October 2018).
2. Suzanne Eller, "#LiveFreeThursday: Why Is It So Hard to Say No?" *Living*

Free Together (blog), March 24, 2016, http://tsuzanneeller.com/2016
/03/24/say-no/#more-11691.

3. Lisa Whittle (@lisawhittle), Instagram, September 29, 2017,
https://www.instagram.com/p/BZo72F_n3jv/?taken-by=lisawhittle.

4. Kristin Wong, "Why You Should Learn to Say 'No' More Often," *New
York Times*, May 8, 2017, https://www.nytimes.com/2017/05/08
/smarter-living/why-you-should-learn-to-say-no-more-often.html?_r=0.

CHAPTER 10: HELP

1. Amanda Palmer, *The Art of Asking* (New York: Grand Central Publishing,
2015), 13, 14, italics in original. While I enjoyed and agreed with parts
of this book, I do not endorse all of Ms. Palmer's views, nor her use of
offensive language.

2. Anne Lamott, *Help, Thanks, Wow: The Three Essential Prayers* (New York:
Penguin, 2012), 15.

3. Lisa Appelo, "In Times of Need: Learning to Receive," *True & Faithful*
(blog), October 21, 2015, http://lisaappelo.com/learning-to-receive/.

CHAPTER 11: WAIT

1. Edmond Stapfer, *Palestine in the Time of Christ* (New York: A. C.
Armstrong and Son, 1885), 256–257.

2. Ruth Chou Simons (@gracelaced), Instagram, August 20, 2017,
https://www.instagram.com/p/
BYCMW58Axdu/?hl=en&taken-by=gracelaced.

CHAPTER 12: WHOLE

1. Thank you for this reminder, Kara Leonino, editor extraordinaire.

2. Bonnie Gray, "Having Mental Health Issues Doesn't Mean You're a Bad
Christian," *Relevant*, August 30, 2017, https://relevantmagazine
.com/article/having-mental-health-issues-doesnt-mean-youre-a-bad
-christian/. Bonnie is also the author of *Finding Spiritual Whitespace*
(Grand Rapids, MI: Revell, 2014), which I highly recommend.

3. After Adam and Eve had first disobeyed God, they hid from him. "The
LORD God called to the man, 'Where are you?'" (Genesis 3:9).

4. *Strong's Concordance*, s.v. "psychē," italics in original.

5. Ann Voskamp, "Do You Feel Broken and Fragmented?" *Q Ideas*,
http://qideas.org/articles/do-you-feel-broken-and-fragmented/.

6. I first proposed this idea in my book *The Happiness Dare* (Carol Stream,
IL: Tyndale House, 2016,) as a way to invite Jesus into all the areas of your
life, "delighting in what brings you delight." See page 26.

CHAPTER 13: REST

1. Mark 1:33
2. Mark 1:37
3. Mark 1:38
4. "How Being Busy Became a Badge of Honor," *MPR News*, March 21, 2016, https://www.mprnews.org/story/2016/03/21/the-drive-to-be-busy.
5. Justin Talbot-Zorn and Leigh Marz, "The Busier You Are, the More You Need Quiet Time," *Harvard Business Review*, March 17, 2017, https://hbr.org/2017/03/the-busier-you-are-the-more-you-need-quiet-time.
6. Ibid.
7. Emma Seppälä, "Happiness Research Shows the Biggest Obstacle to Creativity Is Being Too Busy," *Quartz*, May 8, 2017, https://qz.com/978018/happiness-research-shows-the-biggest-obstacle-to-creativity-is-being-too-busy/.
8. Ibid.
9. See 1 Kings 19:11–12.
10. John 15:4, esv
11. John 15:2, nlt
12. Ibid.

CHAPTER 14: GUARANTEE

1. Proverbs 19:21
2. Psalm 18:30
3. Tim Keller, *Walking with God through Pain and Suffering* (New York: Dutton, 2013), 3, 5.
4. Galatians 5:22–23, nlt
5. *Strong's Concordance*, s.v. "enkráteia."

About the Author

JENNIFER DUKES LEE is also the author of *The Happiness Dare* and *Love Idol*. She is a popular blogger, a writer for DaySpring's (in)courage, and a speaker at women's conferences across the United States. Her words have been featured on numerous podcasts, radio programs, Proverbs 31 Ministries, Fox News *Opinion*, the *Des Moines Register*, and *Today's Christian Woman*.

A former news reporter for several Midwestern newspapers, Jennifer still loves to chase a great story. Nowadays, however, she prefers to write about the remarkably good news of Jesus Christ.

Jennifer is known for her authentic voice, as she encourages women to walk in freedom. She clings to the hope of the Cross and is passionate about sharing the gospel through story. She believes in miracles; she is one. She marvels at God's unrelenting grace for people who mess up—stumbling sinners like her, who have been made whole through Christ.

Jennifer and her husband live on the Lee family farm in Iowa, where they raise crops, pigs, and two beautiful humans. She attends a small country church, where some Sundays you'll find her spinning tunes as the church DJ. She's a big fan of dark chocolate, emojis, eighties music, bright lipstick, and Netflix binges. She wants to live life in such a way that you can't help but want more of Jesus.

Visit Jennifer online at www.JenniferDukesLee.com. She invites you to join her on Twitter and Instagram, @dukeslee, and on Facebook at www.facebook.com/JenniferDukesLee.

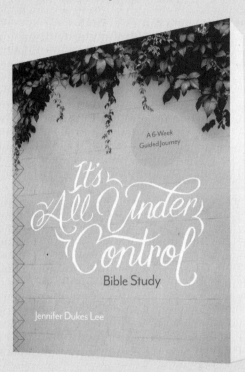

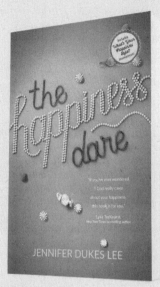
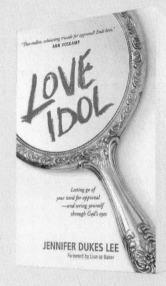